What people are saying about ...

LASTING EVER

"Rebecca and Cubbie's story is a powerful testament to God's faithfulness through life's ups and downs. Their honesty about both the joys and struggles in their journey is refreshing and inspiring. *Lasting Ever* is a story that will remind all of us about how true love endures. This book will encourage anyone seeking to build a life and relationship centered on Christ."

Michael W. Smith, Grammy Award–winning artist

"Rebecca's life has been an open book as she has written, spoken, and sung about her journey from girlhood to womanhood. A whole generation of girls has grown up guided by her words about life, love, waiting for her husband, and godliness all along the way. Now in *Lasting Ever*, she invites us into her new chapter of life and is equally candid about marriage, motherhood, work-life balance, and living her faith in a complex and often confusing world. But—surprise! This book is not a solo story, it is a delightful duet with husband Cub—the man of her dreams who was worth waiting for. Together with equal transparency, they share from both a woman's and a man's perspective about dealing with life's biggest joys, sorrows, and challenges. You are going to love this open book—and them!"

Dr. Wess Stafford, president emeritus of
Compassion International and author of *Too
Small to Ignore* and *Just a Minute*

"Depth, beauty, heart. A few words to honestly sum up the work of two of my favorite people. Call me a biased brother, maybe I am?! But I have also known, traveled the world, laughed, cried, and partnered with my dear sister Rebecca (or as I call her, Jeanie) for half a lifetime, and I have also known my brother-in-law for nearly a decade and a half. And what an honor it has been. Particularly to experience how they, as a power-pair, have partnered on creating a beautiful family as well as safe spaces through movies and music, and now literature, for others to be known, seen, and loved ... Speaking of marriage, never has there been a union closer to Jesus' heart than matrimony. And by continuation of this truth, is there a more holy collaboration than the one between spouses? If there is, I am unaware of it. With all of this said, I am personally so very thankful to now have the insights and stories poured out in these pages, and not without the important formation of hurts and questions and history ... it's all packed into this book. Knowing another's story can be the greatest way to understand our own. Sincerely, from the ever-proud and inspired (and a touch biased) little brother."

Joel Smallbone, For King & Country

"As someone who is single, and looking forward to marriage one day, this incredible book highlighting Bec and Cubbie's story has been a huge encouragement to me. I would recommend it for those in the waiting as well as those who have found their life partner!"

Andrew Bergthold, We The Kingdom

LASTING EVER

REBECCA ST. JAMES
CUBBIE FINK

with Kaley Rivera Thompson and Charis Dietz

LASTING
EVER

FAITH, MUSIC, FAMILY &
BEING FOUND BY TRUE LOVE

DAVID C COOK®

transforming lives together

LASTING EVER
Published by David C Cook
4050 Lee Vance Drive
Colorado Springs, CO 80918 U.S.A.

Integrity Music Limited, a Division of David C Cook
Brighton, East Sussex BN1 2RE, England

Library of Congress Control Number 2024948930
ISBN 978-0-8307-8785-2
eISBN 978-0-8307-8786-9

The Team: Kaley Rivera Thompson, Charis Dietz, Michael Covington,
Stephanie Bennett, Brian Mellema, Jack Campbell, Susan Murdock
Cover Design: James Hershberger
Cover Photography: Robby Klein

Printed in the United States of America
First Edition 2025

1 2 3 4 5 6 7 8 9 10

102824

This book is dedicated to our children,
Gemma, Imogen, and River. It is a delight and
privilege to live this adventure with you!

To Charis Dietz and Kaley Rivera Thompson, our
trusted and beloved partners on this project.

And above all, to God, the author of our lives
and our greatest Love. To Him be the Glory.

CONTENTS

Section Five: LOVED

INTRODUCTION

"Waiting for the look in your eyes,
When we meet for the first time ..."
Rebecca St. James, "Wait for Me"

From that first look where we caught each other's eyes across a crowded room in Los Angeles, there was something magical. Something that teased us with the idea of a romance that could last. Something that made us feel that this song lyric, written many years before by a hopeful, hopeless romantic, was very possibly coming true.

We're here with you in this written moment because we would love to be an encouragement to you. Throughout our marriage, we've thrown around the idea of writing a book. So, when God used a film producer friend of ours to inspire us to authentically talk about both the struggles and the triumphs that have occurred in our faith and family life, we knew it was time.

The concept of *Lasting Ever* comes from the idea that most of us long for the fairy tale, the "happily ever after," love everlasting. But then, life happens. And when it doesn't appear that life is working out for us, we can tend to want to jump ship, blaming and bailing on God, a relationship, or a spouse. We forget that getting to the good stuff spiritually and relationally often involves sticking with our commitments, especially in the hard times. We have learned that the secret of lasting is choosing to endure *together*, through the challenges and joys of our lives.

It's not that the desire for happiness or joy is bad; in fact, we're created to want it. We were made for a perfect garden! And our longing for the "ever after" part is actually longing for something eternal. That also was planted within us. It's just that we were never promised that life would be easy … in truth, we were promised the opposite. "In this world you will have trouble" (John 16:33). So when life gets hard, we have often asked ourselves, why are we surprised?

There's also the question of where we are looking for our happiness. Is it in God and the peace He offers that passes all understanding? Or is it in a person, a human who will often fail us? We have disappointed each other at many points, and this book reflects that, while it also points to a good and gracious Father who redeems, restores, and makes things beautiful in His time.

So here we are, writing about our journeys so far, separately and together, praying that what we share will be a blessing to you.

In the coming pages, we hope you receive encouragement to stand firm and faithful, even when it hurts. May you feel challenged to be brave enough to stay through the hard, holy moments life requires of us.

Here is our love story that's still being written. A story of how we've been found by God's true love at every turn. Let's flip the page together.

Full of hope and faith,
Cubbie and Rebecca

Section One

SEEN

Chapter 1

VOICELESS

Rebecca

I lost my voice.

I know. It is a strange place for a music artist to start a book titled *Lasting Ever*, talking about losing the very thing necessary for her to have a music career. But we must. Why? Because in the backward kingdom of God, it's in the loss that we gain a deeper understanding of God and His gifts. In challenging times we experience Him as the great redeemer and restorer of our stories. **In the secret place of suffering, we discover we are seen, heard, held, known, and LOVED.**

The public spotlight began to shine on me in the early 1990s when I was just thirteen years old. I had the unique opportunity to open for Christian artist Carman in my home country of Australia. A few short years later, I was "seen" by thousands of people when my family moved to Nashville, Tennessee.

I began to take stages in America after I signed a record deal with ForeFront Records and my debut album was released. As a young teenager many eyes were on me, and I'll be sharing how my sensitive heart felt the weight of that in the chapters to come.

But now, I'm forty-six years old and it's a perfect, warm fall day in Louisville, Kentucky. I'm standing side stage watching Kirrilee Berger beautifully play my sixteen-year-old self for the last scene of the movie being made about my family, *Unsung Hero*. The kids and I got here just before this shot, and I'm so grateful we made it in time. I didn't want to miss this conversation between the on-screen versions of my mum and me because this is the capstone moment of the movie. I know that what I'm about to witness is going to be powerful. Shifting my two-year-old son on my hip, I lean in close to my mum, Helen, as we watch the actresses playing us repeat a moment we had experienced hundreds of times in real life. Show after show we would pray before I would go out onstage … prayer was, and still is, my lifeline.

"My dream is to be just like you. You're my hero, Mum," the young version of me says as she heads onto stage to sing at a festival I have played many times in real life, Creation Fest. Hanging in the background of the set is a banner with a logo similar to my tour for my *God* album. Kirrilee looks so identical to me at this age that my dad, David, did a double take when he saw her … for a second he thought she was me.

Emotions roll over me like a tidal wave. I'm smashed by the nostalgia of this moment, and tears begin to stream down my face.

Am I crying because I'm suddenly aware of how surreal it is to watch a young woman play me in a movie? How many people on the planet get to do that?

Are the tears because my mum, now in her sixties, is standing here beside me, not only watching an actress playing her younger self, but witnessing the depiction of one of our tender mother-daughter moments that happened before so many of my shows in real life?

Maybe I'm also incredibly moved because my husband is on the directorial team, capturing this moment in front of our three kids, and I'm hit with the beauty of God's redemption in our family's true story?

Probably all of the above.

Additionally, I wonder if a large part of my heart is thinking about the joy I see in my youthful counterpart (true to that time) as she steps out to sing. The scene being recorded in front of me rolls in slow motion as I think about how much that little girl would experience in the coming years. As if the stage is a time warp, I can visualize young Rebecca walking off as a grown woman, her smile faded, breathless and scared, losing her voice from the trauma of it all.

Even now, so many years later, when I think back to this season of loss in my life, tears well up in my eyes and my stomach clenches. It's still terrifying to acknowledge that my nightmare became real.

Made for More

It is a harsh reality, but our bodies cannot do what they weren't created to do. I found out the hard way that if you spend almost twenty years touring—often packing in interviews, songwriting, recording, and book writing at the same time—you will burn out. If you don't choose to slow down, to Sabbath and rest, God has programmed our bodies to choose that for us. It is both a protection and a consequence.

But before I share how I discovered what I wasn't created for that led to me losing my voice, I want to tell you exactly what I think I *was* created for—through one of the first moments I truly felt seen by God.

I happened upon this discovery at four years old. I was a little girl with tawny curls walking the wide white halls of Hornsby Hospital in the suburbs of Sydney, Australia. Hand-in-hand with my dad, my little heart fluttered with excitement because I had been invited to do something that felt very big: meet the newest member of my family.

After rounding the corner and stopping at a room with a large plate-glass window, my dad lifted me up for a better view of the rows of tiny, bundled babies in their fleet of rolling bassinets. As I pressed my hands and forehead to the glass, I scanned the nursery for one treasure—the one our family would be bringing home.

"That's ours," Dad said, pointing at one of the wrapped presents like it was my real life baby doll. *Ours.* My own baby brother, Ben, had arrived, and I was over the moon when, later in my mum's hospital room, he was placed into my eager little arms.

As the oldest of seven children, a new Smallbone child was added to my family every couple of years until I was fourteen. (Dan was born when I was two, and then came Ben.) I had four more of these first-look moments with brand-new siblings bundled in striped hospital blankets. These moments never lost their wonder for me; something about the experience of holding a newborn in my arms kindled the beginning of the biggest dream of my heart: to become a mother and have my own little ones to hold and care for one day. I knew in my bones that I was made to create and cultivate a family. My family was (and still is) my everything.

I quickly became what my mum called her "right hand." It was a title that filled me with pride. I was capable and responsible. As I watched Mum care for my siblings and find joy in the wild moments that come with raising a busy young family, I emulated her. Feeding, diapering, entertaining, and soothing my baby siblings came so naturally to me.

I distinctly remember moments where mum would be tied up with cooking dinner and a baby would get particularly fussy. My creative brain went right to work filling a laundry basket with pillows and gently placing one of my brothers inside. The mini makeshift crib would be shuffled off into another room where I'd sing a lullaby and rock the basket side to side, sometimes even successfully getting my brother not only content but down for a nap. Victory!

In a bright pink, paper-covered journal with crinkled corners where Mum recorded observations about my young life, I recently found an entry from when I was seven years old:

"My estimation of you at seven years old is that you are a sweet and very sensitive little girl ... You have a strong conscience and endeavor to do the right thing ... You are very truthful. You are also very helpful around the house and very capable in most things that you do. But as you have grown up a bit this last year, you are beginning to object to being asked to do things, but prefer to decide to do the jobs without being asked. You demonstrate leadership qualities and at times can be overpowering in your bossiness. You enjoy school and friends, but enjoy home and feel a great affinity with the home environment."

Mum nailed the fact that I loved to help. The longing of my heart from the jump was to mother and care for a family of my own. No one needed to ask me to watch my little siblings, come up with a game we all could play, or give kisses to soothe a toddler with a bump or scratch. Mothering and caregiving were things I felt like I was born to do.

That's why it was quite an adjustment for me when, a few short years later, we moved to America. I signed a record deal (more on this to come), and my career took over my life for nearly two decades. I once had twelve performances in eleven days on a tour in Europe. Many times, there would be six to twelve interviews in the morning and a concert at night. Often, I would cry worried tears before the beginning of a tour because I just didn't feel I had enough stamina, enough to give.

Although every day was filled with good things like touring, writing, recording, and ministering to God's people across the globe, my primary dream was never to sing. At some point I started to wonder if my career was keeping me from receiving what I'd actually always longed for—a family of my own.

I hope you understand that my intention in sharing is not to have you feel sorry for me. What a high calling I had been given! All these things were thrilling and a privilege in their own ways. So please hear me say that my ministry was one of the biggest blessings of my life. God did remarkable things through these concerts, albums, interviews, books, and performances. It was exhilarating, and the travel was enlightening and life changing. I met and worked with the most beautiful, wonderful people, including many of my family members.

It's just that my heart wasn't made to maintain the pace of my schedule. The Bible says, "Hope deferred makes the heart sick" (Prov. 13:12), and my hopes for my life lay somewhere other than music. But instead of pausing long enough to pursue my dream of finding a husband and having children, I muscled up and pushed through. After all, outside of not knowing what else I would do vocationally until my prince arrived, my family of origin was counting on me. How would they survive if I quit? I kept pressing in until, when I was almost thirty years old singing on a tour with Barlow Girl, I realized that my voice couldn't be pushed anymore.

During my career, I worked with several vocal coaches, so I knew about caring for my vocal cords and avoiding strain in order to sing for extended periods of time. I met with three of them and was assured that my voice was fine. I could do the vocal runs. While on the Barlow Girl tour, I also reached out to one of the singers whom I knew was a vocal coach to ask for tips. After trying everything and hearing repeatedly that my voice was in pretty great condition, I came to realize what I had suspected for a while: Improper use wasn't the cause of my vocal loss; it was the anxious feeling that seemed to relentlessly hover in my gut. It was as if, when I went to sing my songs, my body forgot how to breathe. My whole core felt as if it was straining and I couldn't get any power behind my notes. It was a nontraditional version of a panic attack and, physically and emotionally, I was in serious pain.

I've since traced a root of that anxious feeling back to my formative years, when someone I really cared about told me, "You're not the best singer in the world, but you're a great communicator." While they meant well (and of course I know I'm not the best singer in the world!), my teenage self logged away the words along with an insecurity about what I had to offer vocally. In what they shared, I heard the words "not enough." At the same time, I embraced the thought of effectively communicating a message and I felt confident in that gifting from God.

Honestly, I liked that I didn't have a huge, pop-style or ballad-carrying voice. My sound was unique, and I leaned into it. However, that statement caused a deep-seated insecurity that always stayed with me. Over the years, that seed took root and planted fear deep in my heart. I was terrified that I wasn't enough and that, one day, I wouldn't be able to pull it together onstage. I'd lose it and have to walk off in humiliation.

The fear and anxiety only built, making my voice worse over time. Instead of pausing to work through it, I tried to go around it.

Not Around but Through

I can be a vibey singer, I thought. *I'll just make my notes breathy and it'll be cool.* Truthfully, it wasn't working as I'd hoped. One time in a breakout session at a show in Europe, I was supposed to lead a worship song a cappella. My throat completely clenched up and I couldn't get out more than a squeak. To cover my shameful moment, I invited the audience to carry the tune to the song, hoping they would think I planned it that way.

When my voice was at one of its worst points, I recorded a live album, and if I hear those songs now, I cringe because I can hear my vocal challenges and breathing issues. It was a grace of God that I could creep through songs the way that I did during that season, but I now realize I should have paused to find my strength again.

We've all done this. We'll have an issue continuously pop up in our family, or a sin we think we have repented of but keep repeating, or some obstacle in our path we seem to trip on over and over again. But instead of acknowledging the issue and finding a solution to our problem, we try to skirt around it.

"Oh, my husband and I will eventually stop fighting about that." We ignore our building resentment and optimistically think, *We don't really need to talk about it. Just keep pretending like it's fine and maybe one day it will be.* We lash out at our children in anger and frustration, excusing it because they will just not listen! Or we know God is calling us to a new place of freedom and joy, but we cower in fear, intimidated by our calling and destiny.

What needs to be said (because I needed to hear it too) is this: **You can't keep doing the same thing and expect a different result.**

Joel, my brother, was one of my background singers. He was, and still is, a soul sibling. Sometimes in the middle of a concert we would look at each other. He could read me well and see the agony and fear in my eyes. With his gaze he would communicate, *It's going to be okay. You don't need to be afraid. I've got your back. You can do it!*

Really, we all need to hear this and know that, most importantly, God sets His encouraging, empowering gaze upon us. He, too, sees us in the middle of our struggle and says:

"I will instruct you and teach you in the way you should go; I will counsel you with my loving eye on you" (Ps. 32:8).

Take a moment and notice God lovingly looking at you. He sees your struggle and you can unashamedly meet His eyes, admit your problem, and ask for help.

When we notice that God sees us and ask Him to tackle our issue, His presence enables us to stop circling our problems and walk through them courageously. To live a different life, His best life for us, we may find that God will ask us to do life differently, sometimes dramatically differently.

Doing Different

"I'm taking a job in San Diego. Want to move out there with me?"

One of my good friends had just accepted a job across the country and her question was my lifeline. I believe God prompted her to reach out to me, as I strongly doubt my highly relational self would have ever attempted such a big move and the resulting break of connections alone. God saw my desire to make a big change and to heal, to sow into my love for acting, and to start fresh somewhere new.

My vocal issues were continual with the breathlessness now seeping into my speaking ability. If a relational dynamic was particularly stressful for me, I would struggle to get words out. My body was shouting so loudly at this point I could no longer ignore it. Turning off the mute button in my heart, I decided to let myself finally hear how badly I needed a break and gave myself permission to try something new.

I packed up my bags in Nashville, Tennessee, and unpacked them in Encinitas, California, at an apartment just five miles away from the childhood home of a Jesus-loving bassist named Cubbie Fink, a man my healing heart was beating for who I didn't yet know existed.

Cubbie

As it's affectionately referred to, the "Armpit of California" wasn't exactly a dream spot for my family to settle in after my dad's job moved us from the picturesque mountain landscape of Evergreen, Colorado. I went from watching elk and mule deer graze through the lush meadow just below my grandfather's A-frame cabin, to riding my bike around the suburban, cookie-cutter stucco-covered dwellings of yesteryear, in hot and dusty Bakersfield, California.

While I missed the mountain air, perfect bluebird Colorado skies, and hiking up the hill behind Papa's cabin to sit on a boulder (my moss-covered throne to take in all of God's kingdom), I did eventually find a new sense of boyhood freedom in Bakersfield. Mounting my bike, I would listen to the tires spin at my feet, often with a baseball card fixed between rear spokes, and sing a song to their rhythm. At the top of my lungs, loud enough for the neighborhood to hear as I flew by, I would sing one of my favorite songs at the time, Bruce Springsteen's "Born in the USA" (which I mistakenly pronounced "bomb in the USA").

My memories of Bakersfield are, as is every moment of my childhood, very vivid. Some of my earliest recollections involve lying in my crib and watching my mobile spinning above me. I can recall the texture and how the shag or berber carpets felt in every house we lived in through the late '80s and '90s. As if I put them on yesterday, I know the way my first pair of high-top, dark brown and turquoise with matching nylon laces, hook-closure hiking boots felt as I laced them up on the bottom step of Papa's cabin before setting out on an expedition.

Oddly enough, though, there's a gaping hole in the tapestry of my memories. It's as if there's a space and time in the middle of our brief season in Bakersfield that has been cut out of my brain and removed almost altogether.

Aside from this minor lapse, I remember just about everything. I remember waving to my dad out of multiple windows as he circled the house on his way to work every morning. I remember the small patch of concrete in our backyard where I spent long hours creating chalk drawings. I remember the rough cedar fence that lined the far end of our cul-de-sac. I remember the places the tree roots had pushed up the sidewalk where I rode my bike. I remember the cool shade and smell of the willow tree down the street from our house.

And I remember the day police cars showed up, sirens blazing, to arrest the man who lived across the street from us. He had a family, including a daughter about my age. We had played together, and I had been to her house, and yet what I can't remember is anything from inside that house. After watching the officers handcuff him and shove him into the back of the police car, my parents sat me down to ask, "Did anything strange happen in that house?" To which I replied, "No." Satisfied that we were good, we all moved on with our lives.

Except ... I moved on differently. The bike rides that followed the period in question were a little quieter.

I lost my voice.

Don't Stay Silent

Losing the ability to sing is something Rebecca and I have only recently connected the dots on and have been able to relate over. The ways that our lives parallel are becoming ever more and more mind-blowingly poetic to me. That's why, as I helped direct the final scene of *Unsung Hero* and looked over to see silent tears falling down my wife's cheeks, I had a pretty good indication of what she was feeling.

As a filmmaker, I've been forced to become comfortable with compromising. Not morally, but creatively, because at times it feels like the world is working against you. It's pretty rare to have the opportunity to create and capture something exactly the way you envision it over long months of preparation, when the scenes of a film exist only as black Courier words on a white page. So many moving parts must converge at just the right moment in the midst of the organized chaos that is a film set, to properly catch the magic exactly how it exists in your head.

So when the forecast in Louisville, Kentucky, turned for the worse for the last week of shooting, we began to stare down the reality of one of these aforementioned compromises. For a series of reasons, the decision was made to bump up the day to shoot the final scene of *Unsung Hero*. We woke that morning to yet another of the many miracles we experienced throughout production, beginning our day with rays of sunlight breaking through the parting clouds.

Our focus turned to the feat of recreating an authentic full-scale rendition of a '90s outdoor music festival, which included the herding, placing, and directing of nearly a thousand extras. The several pages of script we needed to film that day culminated in a perfect sunset to backlight Kirrilee Berger (the actress cast as young Rebecca) and Daisy Betts (the actress cast as Helen Smallbone, Rebecca's mom) as they said the film's final lines.

Through a bad pair of headphones and a small director's monitor situated at the front of the stage in the amphitheater, I watched and listened to the scene of Rebecca telling her mom that her dream was never to be a performer, but it was to be just like her ... a wife and mom. After a beat of the two sitting in the weight of the heartfelt admission, Rebecca proceeded to take the stage at Creation Fest with all the joy and excitement in the world. "Cut" was yelled. It was a rare and almost perfect take. The actors were phenomenal, and God gave us a warm golden autumn sunset that, according to the best weather technology, should not have happened. Not only were we not forced to compromise creatively to capture this most important of moments, but we received the gift of a scene that was even better than we had envisioned it.

Tears streamed down my cheeks, and I turned to see my Rebecca standing by the monitors at the opposite end of the stage. Tears ran and dripped from her face. We met center stage and embraced, bonding over the power of this moment. There were so many things we were wordlessly communicating as we cried and held each other.

We both know how incredible her story is. We also know that this beautiful moment full of adolescent joy being acted out in front of us would in reality be replaced with an adult struggle that made her stronger. So much was given, and just as much was taken away—for us both.

Like Rebecca, I didn't lose my voice completely. It's not that I had vocal cord damage or got sick. I simply couldn't find it in my young heart to recall the ability to form words into melodies anymore. "Bomb in the USA" was the favorite song to some distant kid in a faraway time and place. I was no longer him. Someone stole that little boy on a bike and replaced him with a young man who would eventually stand in church and, in a sea of congregants singing in worship, be completely still. Silent.

While I'm still classified as the strong, introverted, and quiet type, I now know that the enemy wins if we stay silent. So, we must start talking about the freedom we experience when we dive into the hard places and face our trauma head-on with Jesus. We must unashamedly share that there is life, joy, freedom, and peace when we decide to walk through our problems guided by the Word of God instead of suppressing them.

We have to take our voices back.

We have to sing again.

Hardship and Harvest

"So I will restore to you the years that the swarming locust has eaten" (Joel 2:25 ESV) is a Bible verse that has recently hung on our fridge. This message has resonated so deeply with us as we have seen restoration, healing, and redemption after years of turmoil where we didn't understand the hurt and pain we carried. Just like the farmer in Joel 2, after seasons of great harvest, we had seen tremendous amounts of loss.

Think with us about this: The farmer in this chapter of Joel has tilled soil, planted seed, watered, waited, and tended to what grew. He harvested and carried his hard-earned bounty to the storehouse, into a place he thought was safe, only for it to be destroyed. This would have been devastating. It could have meant starvation for his family. He would have been asking God questions like we all do in a season of loss.

God, where are You?
What are You doing?
Why would You let something grow only to take it away?
Will You provide where we now lack?
What if there's not enough?

Life has trouble. The locusts will eat. Suffering and loss will come. But Jesus tells us in John 16:33, "Take heart! For I have overcome the world." We have found that God is always up to something, even in our hardship. Here are the two things we know He's up to when we face loss and devastation:

When life yields hardship instead of harvest, God is either supernaturally bringing something deemed useless back to its full potential or He is planning to offer us a greater yield in a new season that makes up for our current lack.

Want to know what we're most inspired by in this story? After the farmer realized his whole crop had been lost, he still got up the next day and put his hand back to the plow to prepare for a new growing season. He had gained wisdom on how to better store his crop and applied that to his work so he could protect it next time. In expectation for the harvest to come, he had to keep working while he waited on God to come through.

Like the farmer, if we want to see God restore what we've lost, we have to put our hand back to the plow. While it may not make sense to us right now, everything we're going through is actually equipping us for all God wants to give us in the future. We have to keep working and walking in God's Word while we wait on Him to come through because, rest assured, He will.

Now, it might not all get happy and bright and shiny and easy. But God will draw us closer to Himself. There is great beauty in our pain and losses in life causing us to rely on Him more deeply. There is joy in His presence even when we have nothing else. We desperately need God when the locusts have eaten. That full reliance on our heavenly Father is a gift.

This is why, in order for you to know how God gave us back our voices and we began to sing again, you have to know about the good seed of music He first placed in our hearts that grew into the devastatingly wrecked but supernaturally replenished harvest of our lives.

Chapter 2

SOUNDS OF MUSIC

Rebecca

My little brother Joel (or "Joely" as I've most often called him) was crying outside his classroom at our Christian private school in Brisbane. He told me that he didn't have friends. I could tell his little heart was sad and lonely. It was his first time attending school, so he was still figuring out kindergarten.

As the oldest child in our family, I didn't have an older sibling to help me navigate my transition into school life. So, I did exactly what I would have given anything for someone to do for me when I was little and school was new and hard. I wrapped my arms around my little brother just outside his classroom. I lightly pushed his auburn hair back in line with his part and wiped the tears out of his eyes. Through our embrace, I softly and simply reminded him, "Yes, you do have friends, and you'll be okay!"

Ironically, a decade and a half later, he would be encouraging me onstage with some of those same words.

That small conversation at school shifted our relationship in a big way. The weeks following our pep talk, Joel was extra sweet and wanted to spend more time with his big sister. That one tender moment connected us for life. This realization inspired me to write these lyrics:

> *Just a little bit o' love goes a long, long way.*
> *Just a little bit o' love'll make someone's day.*
> *Just a little bit o' love, give it away.*
> *God so loved us He gave His only Son.*
> *So we might love each other just as He has done.*
> *He showed us the way to love everyone.*
> *Oh, show His love.*[1]

People Need Music

My first song, "Little Bit of Love," rolled off my pen and onto paper as a way to process all that I learned from that moment with my brother (crazily enough also making the cut onto my first album four years later in 1994). You see, music has always been a natural part of the fabric of my life, as organic to me as breathing. But even more so than loving music has been the innate knowledge from a very young age that people genuinely need songs that inspire. Just like Joel, we all long for encouragement and someone to help us find the words when we don't have them. Music, especially "Jesus music," lifts our hearts, letting us know that we are not alone, that there is hope.

At nine years old, nestled into my bunk in a dark room full of young girls at Pacific Hills Christian School Camp, I sang everyone to sleep. Despite our exhaustion from days full of fun camp activities like trust falls, sailing, and boiling hot water to make tea over an open fire, no one was drifting off to slumberland. We were away from our homes and families, not in our own beds, not in our own rooms. So, my natural next action to soothe our souls to sleep was to sing a soft lullaby.

It could've been "Jesus Loves Me" or another worship song my soul gravitated towards from church at that age. Maybe I did it to meet a need (for all you Enneagram folks, I'm a 2, a helper). Or maybe I regularly did this at home with my brothers. Or possibly it felt like I was Wendy, these were my Lost Girls, and I, as if by magic or fairy dust, could transform the girls' bunk room into a dreamland with just a song.

There is truly a magical quality to music, and I was then, as I am now, thankful to get to be a blessing by using this gift of God.

Divine Setups

Before I tell you more of how the tapestry of music being woven throughout my childhood became the binding threads used to create my future music ministry, here's what I hope you will do as you look at our story and yours:

Pay attention to the way God has been divinely setting you up to uniquely give back what you've been given.

- Who or what has God surrounded you with?
- Can you find some purpose in your placements (the family, towns, churches, and communities you've been a part of)?
- What's that one thing, maybe a desire, dream, or gifting, that has continually surfaced on the pages of your story?

We must closely examine our moments because God's fingerprints are, whether we've noticed them or not, all over our lives. Nothing, not even the hardships and lowest points, are beyond His reach. Setbacks may even have been setups when we look at them through a Holy Spirit–guided lens. So, take a second to step back with me and then Cubbie into our first encounters with music. Think about that one passion God has continuously thrown into your own path—obvious to you now in hindsight—to see how, even if you would've ignored it, you still would have tripped over it.

God has over and again pressed "play" on music in my life. I look back and see how a little Australian girl who gave her gifts and talents to be used by God was all part of a divine setup for me to give songs and lyrics back to the world.

The First Things Are Everything

We were in our normal seats at Thornleigh Community Baptist Church. One of my brothers was coloring on a church bulletin. Another brother, the current baby of the family, was being passed between Mum and Dad. We all stood and began to sing a song in worship, and that's when I noticed Mum had tears streaming down her face. "What's wrong, Mum?" I whispered as I tugged on her dress sleeve. She smiled down at me and in a hushed tone said, "Nothing's wrong, Bec. I'm just overwhelmed by the love of God right now. These are tears of joy."

This was my first memory of really noticing that music can help people connect deeply with God. Worshipping can help us understand that we are extravagantly loved. And from that moment, I longed to experience God like my mum too.

But music wasn't just reserved for church.

Around the table at home, we would often sing grace before meals instead of saying it. It was always the same lines to the same tune and simple enough for the youngest member of the family to master. For always-hungry kids, it was a surely quick way to get to the meal while still giving the blessing! But there was also something powerful about all our voices raised in thanks for God's provision and joy that came from gratitude.

Thank You, Lord, for giving us food.
Thank You, Lord, for giving us food.
Thank You, Lord, for giving us food,
Right where we are,
Amen!

I always had a dream of being "in" *The Sound of Music*. I had watched the movie countless times and a stage version of it as a child and it ignited a love for acting ... and maybe some idealism around singing together as family. I'm not sure if he was clued into this or not, but sometimes at family reunions, our dad, David Smallbone, would ask us kids to sing a parting song for everybody. Yes, very reminiscent of "So Long, Farewell" ... the scene on the stairwell! Maybe Dad was being prophetic and saw a future where we were an Australian version of the Von Trapp Family Singers.

At that time, our growing family accompanied Dad to nearly all the Sydney concerts he promoted in the late '70s and '80s. He had a record label and pro-motions company and would recruit mostly American Christian music artists to perform around Australia. Drawn to musical pioneers who combined gospel-centered lyrics with rock and pop music, Dad filled Australia's stages with the sounds of Christian artists. He brought in bands like Stryper, Whiteheart, and Petra, keen instrumentalists like Phil Keaggy, pop artists like Amy Grant, and theatrical storytellers such as Carman.

Peeking out from behind the curtains at those shows, my brothers and I were able to sing along because these same songs had been spinning on the record and cassette players in our home. But there, amidst live audiences, we were seeing the power of music and the message of a song as it was offered as an act of worship before a crowd. Our family was a part of it, impacted by it, and connected to each other through it.

We would often sing to amuse ourselves on long family car trips. With no phones or screens, the world back then was simpler, and I'm grateful to have experienced it. In fact, it was on a road trip that I first learned to harmonize. My teacher at the time was my uncle Ian Smallbone, a singer in a popular Australian Gospel trio "Family," which my dad managed for a time.

"Take two steps up for the first harmony and then another two steps up for the other harmony," Uncle Ian instructed. It was a simple explanation but made sense to a little girl who had taken piano lessons for a while. I had a natural ear for music and also a bit of a knack for picking up a tune or a recent hit after one listen.

My dad used to watch *Molly Meldrum's Countdown*, showing the music videos of the top ten songs in Australia each week. I would listen in, and he would observe which chorus I would subconsciously start singing while playing or doing chores. Often, it was the top song in the nation at that time. I know for sure that those '80s pop songs influenced my sense of melody and informed my songwriting in my teens and beyond.

When I was twelve, I gave my gifts and talents to God. I wasn't sure how He could use this little Aussie girl to make a difference in the world, but I sure wanted to serve Him in ministry. Around that time, my eighth-grade teacher asked me to try out for the junior rock band at my Christian school, which was made up of students at least a couple of years older than me. Nervous but excited about the possibility, I chose Petra's "Don't Let Your Heart Be Hardened" as my audition song. Simple, sincere, heartfelt—the rendition would earn me a spot as the youngest member of the band.

I also became part of a recording group of students from school, led by another teacher, that resulted in demo recordings for me. Who knows how history might have been different had those two teachers not believed in me and seen something special. I love looking back and seeing how God was shaping the story of my life!

This opening at school seemed to be my first step through the door of music ministry, as shortly after that, I was asked to go on my first tour. Christian artist Carman was looking for an opening act for the Australian leg of his tour. Dad had worked with Carman in the past, successfully promoting his concerts, and true to form, he had brought our family to many of Carman's shows.

Carman was a hero to me, and I greatly looked up to him. With youthful energy he got down on my level but also spoke to me like an adult, treating me with kindness. In his shows, he often depicted the victory of Christ over darkness and the devil in imaginative ways, including a Rocky Balboa–style knockout boxing-match number called "The Champion" (which my brothers and I may or may not have reenacted a time or two in our living room). Audience members were taken in by his larger-than-life storytelling style, but maybe none more so than me.

Naturally, I was excited when Dad told me he had played one of my demo recordings for Carman and he responded, "She should be the opening act for my Revival in the Land tour in Australia." The plan was for me to open each concert with three well-known worship songs, accompanied by Carman's keyboard player. Dad helped me rehearse months beforehand on the stage of our small neighborhood chapel. His theory: *If you can perform well in front of me, you can do it in front of an audience of strangers.* And he proved to be right.

The night of the first show of the tour in Perth, I literally got on my face before God backstage and said, "Lord, if You don't give me strength to go out there, there's no way I can do this!" And God *did* give me the strength to walk out onto the stage each night. As a thirteen-year-old, I learned to rely on the Jesus I was singing about as I toured across Australia and sang in front of crowds of up to six thousand people.

When I trace God's fingerprints now, I can see there was something prophetic about choosing "Don't Let Your Heart Be Hardened" as my audition song for the junior rock band. Though I couldn't have realized it then, keeping a child-like earnestness to please the Lord would be crucial to navigating the pressures of my very public, future ministry. A soft heart would help me stay grounded and connected to my roots of faith, love, and family.

These very things that inspired me to pen my first song would lead me to write, sing, and bring music to the world in the decades to come.

Cubbie

I'm very grateful God's hand was on my young life. I've had my fair share of broken bones and ER visits, so there's really no other logical explanation for how I survived far too many Beavis and Butthead/Jackass/X Games and simply stupidity–inspired ventures and antics over the years. While tamer in comparison, that "Hand" was still upon me the many times I ascended a rickety old ladder to pull my nine-year-old self up into the attic rafters of our San Diego garage.

I would stand on the very tips of my toes in my bright white Reebok Pump tennis shoes and grab hold of a two-by-four to pull myself into another universe. This wasn't just a space to stash discarded clutter above our cars; the attic was a portal that shot me through a stale-air-filled wormhole and into the open wooden beams and plywood that held treasures from my parents' old world. As soon as I landed, I'd take in the various vintage surfboards, a couple of Dad's old drum kits, handcrafted artwork by my mom, and other odds and ends that were collecting dust. Dressed in an outfit of bright neon green DayGlo shorts, matching orange, green, and yellow surfer T-shirt, and a bright pink and blue nylon Billabong ball cap, I was a child-sized highlighter standing amongst the shadows and fading furniture.

As I worked my way through the gems of a bygone era, I was drawn to a large crate of LPs that sat beside a stack of old, forgotten boxes. Kneeling and thumbing through the records, I was mesmerized by the album photos and artwork that seemed to capture a mythological time and place for which I had no frame of reference. About midway through the stack, I stopped at a faded album jacket that displayed four dudes in turtlenecks and shaggy bowl cuts, not exactly sure what about that cover seemed to supernaturally draw me in ... *Wonder what these guys are all about.* The turtleneck dudes were curiously intriguing enough to spark my curiosity to start fishing out the turntable that was collecting dust in the next box.

After nearly slipping and falling my way to yet another visit to the ER, I managed to wrestle the record player, and my new bowl-cut buddies, down that death trap of a ladder, out of the garage, and into my bedroom.

On the floor of my room, I plugged in the record player and blew off the vinyl. Dust bunnies flew into the air like confetti in some sort of prophetic celebration that I was about to discover love at first sound. Now flat on my chest after a couple of somewhat abrasive failed attempts, I eyed up the edge of the spinning record, and the needle finally caught the first groove as I gently let it go.

The moment of anticipation undergirded by a handful of pops and crackles eventually gave way to the opening guitar riff, bass lick, and drum fill of "Drive My Car" ... I was transfixed. *So this is what music can be!* I had discovered the Beatles and *Rubber Soul*, the soundtrack that opened up a whole new porthole for me into the world of music.

By the time I approached my tenth birthday, I worked my way through the entire crate of records and turned my attention to my parents' CD collection. I got hung up in the "J" section of the catalog for a while and wore down more than a few CDs of the legendary, mind-melting, shredder of a guitarist Eric Johnson.

At that point, I became desperate to get an axe of my own. I knew the exact model and could picture how cool I would feel playing the beautiful, sea-foam blue, 1950s-vibe Fender Stratocaster that hung on the top row at the music store Dad and I frequented. So, I took my request to the people that all children go to when they're going to ask for the moon—Mom and Dad.

I knew that my dad, Ed, and mom, Patrice, would surely get it. Live music had always been a part of our world. My dad was a surfer-drummer who some-where along the line received the nickname "ShrED." Seems only fitting for the true godfather of nickname giving to end up with one himself. He has fashioned and bestowed an endearing moniker on just about everyone in his life, including yours truly.

When I was born with a head full of dark hair, thinking I looked a little like a newly born bear cub, he called me "Cubbie." If I'm any indicator, his nicknames tend to stick. I met a fair amount of the possessors of these nick-names while joining Dad on numerous band rehearsals and gigs around town. Watching my dad "shred" was a thrill that never really got old for me as a kid. While I always enjoyed messing around on his drums, he knew how fascinated I was by the rowdy and raw sounds of the electric guitar.

When my tenth birthday rolled around, I was handed a giant box that I knew could only be the Stratocaster of my dreams. A flurry of wrapping paper went flying to unveil ... a small, black, three-quarter-scale, off-brand electric guitar that read "Memphis" on the Jackson-esque headstock. *Hmm.* To my dis-may, Mom and Dad had decided on a learner guitar from the discount section and an eight-inch-tall practice amp that was powered by a 9-volt battery. *Cool.* At that moment, the only good thing I could see about my new setup was at least the "Memphis" had a whammy bar.

A bargain-bin guitar turned out to be a wise parental move, because I was shocked when I started playing and realized I wasn't an instant professional. Everything else in my life had come to me pretty easily—from throwing and hitting a baseball, to riding a surfboard—and I had this idea in my head that guitar would be no different. I honestly thought that if I just strummed the strings fast enough and moved my fingers up and down the neck of the guitar, it would sound amazing, just like Eric Johnson. Guess what? It did not.

Thoroughly disappointed, I set that guitar down in the corner of my room and didn't pick it up again for two more years.

Embrace Failure

When I finally picked up my electric guitar again, I realized that I was choosing for the first time to willingly embrace failure. The finger movements and placements of the chords didn't come naturally to me. I was deciding to be okay with messing up a lot. Horrible notes were about to be played. My ears, fingertips, and ego were going to hurt a little bit. But I knew the outcome of finally learning this instrument was going to be worth it.

If you feel like you're failing today, I want to give you the advice my dad gave to me: "Hang in there. One day it's just going to click. Keep going until it does." Which is similar to the wisdom offered to us in Proverbs 24:16, which says, "For a righteous man may fall seven times and rise again" (NKJV).

One of the great things about being a child of God is that we can know our failures aren't proof that we are a failure. It's just evidence that we're trying. There is grace as we make mistakes trying to figure out new things. We're going to stumble while walking with Jesus, and He's okay with catching us and pointing us back down the correct path.

If you don't have it figured out, just remember that God does. Hang in there. It's going to click. Keep going.

Making Music

Dad was right. After many hard lessons in the back room of our local guitar shop, and even more hours trying to piece together the things taught in those lessons, it all finally did click. My fingers naturally, from muscle memory, danced to the correct strings to form chords and pluck out melodies. The sound swelling from the bargain-bin guitar didn't sound so cheap. I can imagine a smile forming across Dad's face as he stood outside my closed bedroom door and listened to me practice. His little cub was learning the ways of shred.

With his encouragement, I began sitting in on the rehearsals I had previously been accustomed to observing. I was the youngest in these groups by a good thirty years, but I did my best to hold down the guitar in the many classic rock and blues tunes we played. The memories we made eventually playing live shows together at all kinds of venues and settings—from restaurants to car shows, to full-blown surf festivals—were irreplaceable. It was the good life.

While simultaneously playing Led Zeppelin, Eric Clapton, Buddy Guy, Jimi Hendrix, and Eagles covers with my dad, I also started a prog rock band we called Lumineux (meaning "light" or "luminous" in French) with a few of my friends from school. We were surprisingly good for a bunch of high school sophomores who practiced in our drummer's converted chicken coop. Good enough to win Battle of the Bands at our school of over twenty-five hundred kids.

During my senior year I discovered the instrument that was most "me," the instrument that would guide me into my adult life: the bass. I had since helped form a new band that we called "speaking of asLan." Get it? We capitalized the "L" not only because it looked cool, but truth be told, we were mistakenly called "speaking of asian" one too many times. With a slowly growing following, and gigs on the books, our bass player decided to inform us that he was giving up on music to pursue his true passion: computers. Okay? With few options and shows rapidly approaching, I volunteered to fill in until we found a new guy. As history would prove, I was the new guy.

What I discovered was this: If guitar is what you hear, bass is what you feel. It's more of a warm and comforting presence in a room as opposed to the flickering light bulb that grabs your conscious attention. In reality, the bass controls the harmony of a song and dictates how a song is perceived and felt. Bass has more of a subconscious role, and it seemed to fit well with me as a person. I've never been the guy jumping up on the table saying, "Look at me!" I'm more of the person who creates and supports the environment. The bass opened up a whole new world for me and almost immediately became my soul instrument. I immediately felt more of an ability to be naturally expressive on it than I ever did on the guitar, I think because of the way it resonated deep in my core. However, my guitar roots definitely affected the way I approached the bass. The way I thought about and played it was from more of a melodic standpoint rather than approaching it as an instrument that just "held down the roots." I fell in love with all things bass … and at the end of the day, you've got to admit, the bass is just cool.

While playing shows and gigs was a blast, I fell in love with the making of music beyond the performance of it. Some of my fondest moments as a young musician were when our two-hour practices would turn into four- or five-hour jam sessions. Our little blues-rock band, with my dad behind the drums, would take on a soul of its own as we'd find ourselves exploring the space in between the notes. A three-minute blues standard would evolve into a thirty-minute masterpiece as we passed the proverbial spotlight back and forth for poignant moments of melodic and rhythmic declarations. I felt the most joy when we weren't overthinking it and gave each other permission to just get truly lost in the music.

There is something profound about having the ability to create, be it music or any artistic or intellectual expression. In its purest form, I think we get a glimpse of the joy God must feel as He creates, and the joy He finds in His creation. It was there in the songs we shared, yet all played so uniquely, that we felt united in the process of creating in the ways we were created to.

Making music is fellowship, and that raw togetherness is what we all need.

Chapter 3

BACK TO THE BEGINNINGS

Cubbie

About midway through junior high, I began to ask a lot of questions like:

Why should I feel compelled to buy the latest polo shirt from Abercrombie and Fitch?

Why should I trust what the people standing at the front of a classroom are pushing?

Who really decides what is truly right and wrong?

Is there really only ONE way to salvation?

Do I really believe what my parents have told me my whole life about faith, the Bible, and Jesus?

I guess you could say I was deconstructing before it was the cool thing to do. Along with a growing list of questions came a growing desire to do things differently. A desire to not just do things because "that is the way they are done." In its simplest expression, it was a refusal to buy, like, or listen to what was playing on top 40 radio at the time. And in its most abstract representation, it was a refusal to tie my shoes. Haha, weird, I know.

In the midst of this seemingly solo journey and exploration, I met a guy who was asking similar questions and had a similar inclination to "stick it to the man." From the end of junior high and into the first couple years of high school, this eventual best buddy, Colin, and I shared a very specific afterschool ritual:

1. Throw backpacks down in the entryway at Colin's house.
2. Head straight for the kitchen.
3. Load plates with tortilla chips and pile liberal amounts of shredded cheddar cheese on top of said chips.
4. Microwave briefly.
5. Head upstairs to Colin's room.
6. Put Led Zeppelin's "Stairway to Heaven" on record player.
7. Lie on floor with plate of microwaved nachos on your chest and bask in the glow of the moment.
8. Repeat tomorrow.

Epic, right? I know. And we loved it. There was one woman who watched us rinse and repeat this nacho and inspiration routine, and that was Colin's mom, Chris.

Chris was boisterous when she chose to be, but often a quiet observer. If she wasn't closing a deal in their home office, she almost always had her nose in a book when we'd walk in the door. Occasionally she'd peer over the top of said book and insert a thoughtful question, or we would get her laughing with our foolish teenage antics, nothing too serious—with one notable exception.

Midway through freshman year, Chris put her book down and met me in the kitchen mid-nacho assembly and, to put it lightly, called me out. I had figured out a way to maintain good grades by doing the absolute bare minimum, but I was utterly apathetic toward school. I hated reading, and it was plain that—while I was fairly intelligent and capable—there was no fire in me to learn or grow, or to take advantage of the 100 percent free education offered to me by the self-sacrificial educators not doing it for the "glory" of a $30K-a-year salary, but because they were passionate about inspiring young minds. That afternoon, Chris chose her boisterous moment and said her piece.

I was hovering over my plate of freshly microwaved cheese and tortilla chips when Chris, straight and simple, asked me, "What are you doing with your life?" I stopped crunching mid-bite in an effort to avoid choking while she continued. "You are smart and gifted, and you are absolutely missing it. There are teachers in your life ready to give you their full attention, to impart knowledge and wisdom. There is opportunity all around you. Don't waste it."

Chris punched me in the gut. In the best way. Honestly, I needed someone who would be bold enough to see my lethargy clearly and say something. Her rebuke hurt a little, but I could tell she cared about me. She wasn't trying to just call me out, she was calling me up. I had always respected her intelligence and unique perspective on life, so her words carried real weight in my young soul.

What was *I doing with my life?* I didn't have an answer to her question, and now I needed to find one. I immediately began reading anything I could get my hands on. I started engaging in discussions with teachers and enrolled in AP classes. And soon I realized I had even more questions than I thought I had before. But there was one question, *the* question, I could never seem to get a satisfactory answer to: *Why am I here?*

There it was. At the root of the apathy and listlessness was an unfulfilled longing for purpose.

Hear That?

At seven o'clock on a Sunday morning, the roar of galloping horses sounded through our living room—actually (of course) it was the intro to Michael W. Smith's 1990s hit "Go West Young Man." It served as the theme song to our family's "get ready for church" routine.

"But I'm asking for the will to fight, to wear the crown of life, and you say go, go west young man ..." I hummed as I put together some of my favorite thrift-store finds for an outfit: the perfect combination of a four-pocket guayabera shirt, bad polyester pants, and geriatric-style white sneakers with Velcro closures. I discovered that the less on trend the outfit, the cooler I felt.

While Mom and Dad always modeled Christian principles for me and my little sister, Joslyn, they never forced us to declare a decision to follow Jesus. They seemed to just trust that the seeds of truth planted and all those Bible verses Mom lovingly had me memorize would bear fruit in time. But the time hadn't come for me yet. I still didn't know Jesus like they knew Jesus. I just didn't get it.

As a high school freshman, newly turned on to scholarly pursuits thanks to Colin's mom, I searched for answers in history and culture. I searched for a way of life looking to world religions and philosophy, cherry-picking the ideas that most appealed to me from Hinduism, Buddhism, and other Eastern religions with the hope of assembling an existence that would put me at peace with myself and the world around me.

Unfortunately, instead of becoming enlightened, I became more lost than ever. Instead of peace, I found depression ... pretty dark depression. *What is the point of my life?* There were days that I actually thought it would be easier to cease to exist than keep struggling through the pain and confusion of figuring out the point of it all. *Is it this hard for everyone? Why does the meaning of life have to be so complicated?*

All the while, the church that my parents loved so dearly always welcomed me and my questions. I would begrudgingly "tag along" to church, and most frequently joined my parents in the main service. I finally obliged their weekly encouragement to check out the youth group and found my way down the narrow outdoor corridor behind the main chapel to the room where the youth gathered on Sunday mornings. Crossing the threshold of the youth room for the first time, I was met by two things, almost simultaneously: the opening track to Jars of Clay's first album blasting through the speakers of a small boom box near the door, and a bone-crushing handshake from the man who would ultimately help pull me out of the pit of despair I found myself in.

It was a radical encounter with a person who had something I had never experienced before. It wasn't just his kind and gentle blue eyes that seemed to peer deep into my soul and beg the question, "How are you really doing?" It was the fact that I truly felt seen and appreciated by those nearly translucent eyes. There was something different about him. Something genuine. Something real. What I didn't see, or refused to see at the time, was that the difference in him was Jesus. Regardless of my interpretation, it provided enough intrigue for me to at least feel comfortable to start hanging on the periphery of the youth group through my season of questions.

In the couple years that followed my initial interaction with Chris Smaltz, he was always intentional in making me feel like my presence was appreciated. He was never heavy handed, but consistently invited me to things like beach hangs, pool days, or youth camps, to which I slowly grew more willing to say yes. Although, there was one invitation that my immediate response was simply, "No thanks." The ask was to join a small group that would be attending a three-day worship conference near downtown San Diego. Not only did I have multiple commitments over that weekend, things I had been looking forward to and had no intention of missing, but at that point in my journey, going to something like that sounded close to torture.

While my trust in Chris, and genuine intrigue about whatever it was that he had, was growing, I was still buried under a mountain of confusion and depression. A mountain that was founded on my doubt in "The Faith" and my distrust in the expressions of that faith. So a worship conference was pretty much at the bottom of the list of things I would have sought out or desired to attend. To this day, I still don't really know how I ended up agreeing to hop into that fifteen-seater van headed due south for San Diego.

Purpose

Midway through the first song of the first set of the conference, I found myself flat on my face in a puddle of tears—a reaction to hearing what felt like the audible voice of God speak so clearly that I was tempted to look around for the source. In a season of seeking complex and heavily analytical answers to increasingly more complex questions, the words were profoundly simple and exactly what I needed to hear. The simple truth cut through the fog hovering over my brain and depression closing in on my soul. Like a perfectly thrown dart, the statement nailed the bullseye on answering the long-held question in my heart:

"I put you here to worship Me, and to show others how to worship Me."

There it was—purpose. No words are adequate enough to describe the rightness, safety, and all-encompassing love embedded in the way the Holy Spirit speaks, but that sacred sense is what surrounded and overwhelmed me in that moment. Suddenly, the heaviness in my soul was lifted. For the first time in as long as I could remember, I felt free. I had finally met Jesus.

Rebecca

I truly had a great childhood. Being part of a large, close family was a joy to me! We always had someone to talk to, use our imaginations with, and care for. I loved hide-and-seek, playing house, and dressing up. (Little did I know I was prepping for some acting in my future!) In the forest behind our house, I'd reenact scenes from *Star Wars* with my brothers. We would explore the creek and build BMX bike tracks in the fields. It was magical! We'd also put on shows for our parents. I was generally the lead singer with the hairbrush, and there were pots and pans for drums—and always guitars. We even sold merch at our "shows"!

We were so entrenched in the world of concerts that all this was second nature. (I attended my first show at six weeks old in the Sydney Opera House.) Dad promoting concerts meant we were going to shows every month or two. We'd be put to bed on sleeping bags in dressing rooms backstage, listening to the booming bass in the music venue just a few walls away. I listened attentively to the words of the Christian music I was hearing. They were seeds of faith being planted in my little heart.

My life was forever changed at the age of eight, in our small church in the suburbs of Sydney. I was attending Girls Brigade (an Australian version of Girl Scouts), and the speaker was describing to a room full of us preteen girls what Jesus endured on the cross. I have always had a great fear of physical pain, yet here was a God who opted to endure so much torment just to be close to me. Here was Jesus—real, present, and worthy of my whole heart.

All of a sudden, it clicked that Jesus truly did love me. I knew He loved and died for the whole world, but in that moment, I knew Jesus died for *me*. When the speaker extended an invitation for any of us to come forward, I stood and gave Jesus my whole heart.

Later that night, I told Mum everything I had just experienced. "It makes me cry when I think about how much Jesus loves me." This time, we cried tears of joy and love, together.

I changed after that experience with God. In my childhood journal, Mum wrote this: "I noticed this evening that there was an even more lovely spirit in your actions and that you were even more sincere about your desire to please and do the right thing." I love how the Holy Spirit changes and recreates us!

My coming to know Jesus sparked a genuine curiosity about stories of heroes of the faith. A documentary film about the ministry of Mother Teresa and the Missionaries of Charity to the so-called "untouchables" in the slums of Calcutta made the deepest impression on me. She became a hero of mine. I devoured books about men and women who wanted to be of service to the Lord, people who lived for something bigger than themselves. I read stories about Corrie ten Boom and her family's efforts to hide Jews in their home during the Holocaust, and English missionary George Müller's creation of the Bristol orphanage, where thousands of children received care during his lifetime alone.

I could picture myself running my own orphanage one day, tucking rows of children into their bunks every evening. Hadn't helping with my younger siblings already partly trained me for a calling like that?

A few years later, I recall being eager to be used by God, but honestly, I didn't know how or what He would do with my life. What I knew then, though, and even more so now, is that my life orbits around longing to be a part of a grand story, something I could never make up on my own. More than anything, I wanted to be useful, living His great and adventurous plan for me.

I began praying, "Lord, I know I'm young, but I want my life to count, to make a difference in this world. I want to live on mission with You. I don't know how You can use my gifts or talents, but I give them back to You. Use my life."

THE GIFT OF BEING SEEN

Tears fall easily as I think about what I want to share from my heart to yours right now. When I think about the unconditional love and grace God has shown me in my life, it moves me beyond what I can put into words. Mainly because I'm admitting that the lie I've struggled with for most of my life is that I'm not enough. Maybe you're not an onstage performer like Cubbie and me, but you've had someone more or less say to you that you're not good enough, strong enough, hardworking enough, skilled enough, attractive enough ... Why would God look at us when we're not something wonderful to behold? Why would He so freely give His love when we haven't earned it?

The truth is that God has had His eye and heart set on us before we were ever born. Before I ever sang a tune. Before Cubbie longed for purpose in his life. Before any of us ever did anything at all, God looked upon us and, in His grace, loved and continues to love us.

The truth that God has been speaking to my heart is this—being seen and cherished by God is a gift, never something we earn. We do not need to perform well enough to achieve an admiring glance from our Creator. We've been the apple of His eye since we were conceived in our mothers' wombs.

Psalm 139:13–16 so wonderfully sums this up by saying:

"For you formed my inward parts; you knitted me together in my mother's womb. I praise you, for I am fearfully and wonderfully made. Wonderful are your works; my soul knows it very well. My frame was not hidden from you, when I was being made in secret, intricately woven in the depths of the earth. Your eyes saw my unformed substance; in your book were written, every one of them, the days that were formed for me, when as yet there was none of them." (ESV)

The beauty of looking back—at our childhoods, beginnings in music, and the moments we encountered Jesus—is that we can now clearly see God's gaze was upon us. His look of endearment was not a result of anything we could ever do; He chooses to look through the lens of love at us all.

The fact that God sees all of me and yet loves me anyway wrecked me at fifteen, as it does now. So much so that I wrote a song way back then called "Psalm 139." When I was a nervous teen taking her first wobbly steps out into the music industry, it was as if God gave me this verse and song as a reminder of His abounding love for me that was not contingent on my performance. To Him and through Him, I was enough just as I was.

You, too, are enough, just as you are.

In case you need to hear it the way I needed to hear it, here's my song "Psalm 139":

You search me
You know me
You see my every move
There's nothing I could ever do
To hide myself from You

You know my thoughts
My fears and hurts
My weaknesses and pride
You know what I am going through
And how I feel inside

But even though You know
You will always love me
Even though You know
You'll never let me go
I don't deserve Your love
But You give it freely
You will always love me
Even though You know[2]

The fact that God sees us is a gift that is lasting ever. We cannot change the fact that He adores us. But we can decide where we choose to fix our eyes as a result.

- Will we dare to look back at the God who loves us wholeheartedly?
- Will we decide to remain just as steadfast and faithful to Jesus when life is hard and scary and we cannot see the next step ahead?

I often say to my kids, "Look at my love eyes." What I'm actually saying is "See the tenderness in the way I look at you." When we truly see God, we behold the tenderness in His gaze as He beholds us, flaws and all. The God of the universe sees us, knows us, and loves us despite our mistakes and messes.

After knowing what God's "love eyes" look like, we may be curious enough to discover how beautiful and powerful it is to not only be seen but also heard by the unchanging, never-failing God of the universe.

HEARD

Chapter 4

CULTURE SHOCK

Rebecca

There is no sofa, no chairs, no furniture of any kind to sit on in the wide-open living room of our first rental home in Brentwood, Tennessee, a suburb of Nashville. So, when Mum and Dad called their six kids together for a family meeting in the fall of 1991, we sit cross-legged on the light brown carpet—waiting for what, we're not sure.

In the movie *Unsung Hero*, Mum sets a big glass jar down onto the carpet in the center of the group. It holds a small pile of coins topped by a few folded bills. With one hand resting on her growing, pregnant belly, she looks around the circle of faces with wide but trusting eyes. "This is all we have," she tells her crew, gesturing toward the jar. "It will grow, and it will shrink, but it cannot be allowed to disappear." Our reactions are somber but not fearful. We're watching Mum and Dad's faces for cues. And what we see is two parents who have decided that the way forward is transparency, vulnerability, and total reliance on God together as a family.

"We're going to pray, like we've never prayed before, asking and believing for exactly what we need." They may not have chosen this path for their family, but—one way or another—they're going to walk down it with faith and hope together.

The Jar Half Full

Though there was no money jar in real life (we simply sat on the floor as a family to pray), almost all the details of this story are true. This scene represents a season in my life when I truly learned that God does indeed hear us when we pray.

Earlier that year at age thirteen, I had successfully completed my Australian tour opening for Carman and, with Dad's encouragement, had laid down tracks for my first album, a simply produced praise and worship record called *Refresh My Heart*. Only a year or two prior, my dad's career as a concert promoter had been at an all-time high. But when a particularly big tour Dad was promoting did half the previous tour's numbers, the result was financial disaster for his business and a devastating blow to his reputation in the music industry.

We lost our beautiful, modern, brick home in the outskirts of Sydney and our life savings. The doors that had been flung wide open began to close, and long-time partners began to back out of agreements. As a young teen, I was reasonably aware of everything going on but didn't feel overly concerned. My parents had never let us down and I trusted they'd pull us through all the changes. While I could read between the lines of some of my parents' conversations and knew that our family was undergoing hardship, I really wasn't worried. Having successfully brought over and toured many popular American Christian artists up to that point, Dad turned his focus to calling on relationships in the US for work. He struck an arrangement with a past client and friend who agreed to bring him on as his promoter in the States for a season. Eight international flights were purchased for us to cross the pond, only for the artist to reconsider and pull out of the agreement at the last minute. Ever the go-getter, Dad was soon able to secure another job, managing another Christian artist. It seemed like things were going to pan out. It was going to be all right.

We officially entered America in the ideal location of Honolulu, Hawaii. The customs agent, however, was less than welcoming and thought it was strange that we were eight people traveling with fifteen bags, so they flagged us for secondary security. At fourteen, I was old enough to know this was not good. These stern customs agents had the power to send us back to Australia and deny us entry. I saw the dreams I'd had of spending two years on a great adventure in a country that held places like Disneyland potentially all going away. In the movie, our youngest brother, Josh, burst into tears in the customs area, but in real life it was me. Thankfully, the agent found a note from my Nanna in one of our bags that confirmed our short-term stay and we were in!

After landing on the West Coast, our family visited for a week with Aussie friends who lived in San Diego. We explored the harbor, had fish and chips, and played lots of *Super Mario* on their Nintendo. In the early nineties, traveling by rail was still cheaper than by flight for transporting eight people across the country. So, armed with Amtrak train tickets for all, we began to snake a path across North America's heartland, continuing toward our new home.

While it wasn't the most comfortable or efficient situation by any stretch of the imagination, there were highlights for me about our journey. One of my favorite parts of traveling across the country by train was going to the upper level and sitting in the viewing car where there were floor-to-ceiling windows. I have vivid memories of going through mountainous regions and observing the flat prairies of Kansas stretching on and on and on. I felt like a pioneer, surveying the territory of this new country. There was indeed something wondrous about the journey for me. When we finally got off the train in Memphis, I sang "Walking in Memphis," a new hit at the time, as I strolled across the train platform. I was dancing with excitement all the way to the Nashville suburbs, but when our crew finally pulled up to our rental house, we were met with a shock.

It was clear that we were nowhere close to Disneyland when we opened the door of our new home to find the rooms bare, the home completely unfurnished. Always resourceful, Mum pulled all the winter clothes out of the suitcases and transformed them into sleeping pallets by folding them up and covering them with the sheets we brought from Australia. While we were surprised, none of us kids were really upset about what we lacked. For us, this was a good challenge. We had a blank canvas and were able to get creative with how to fill it. The boys played cricket in the house with the bat and balls we brought, and we found a cheap air hockey game that we placed in the empty entry hall. It was a fun and adventurous time for us! Things were looking up, until they weren't. News of Dad's tour not doing well had traveled across the globe and the second artist to hire him let him go.

My parents were always honest with us about our family's lack and Dad's employment struggles. This amazes me because they could have hidden it all in an effort to save their own pride or protect us from reality, but they didn't. They believed we were a team and approached the challenges with a sense of adventure. So, all of us kids were invited into the hardship in a way that allowed us to jump in on the action, seek God, and work together on behalf of each other. This taught me how to seek Jesus and gave us all a front row seat to witnessing undeniable miracles.

Sleeping on beds of clothes with few groceries, no car, very little cash, and now no income, our entire family began to pray very specifically for provision. And God heard us. We prayed for work opportunities to earn money. The boys raked and bagged leaves and Mum and I cleaned a few homes in the neighborhood, and God turned it into an enterprise of a full-family yard maintenance and house cleaning crew. I used my second mum-of-the-family skills and went to work babysitting consistently for church friends and neighbors. Every dollar bill and coin earned went into the family's cash stash. There was no hesitation, no second thoughts, just a sense of pride among us kids who were contributing in a tangible way and got to see up close as God was answering our prayers.

We prayed for food. God laid it on the heart of a neighbor lady to buy extras for us sometimes when she went to the grocery store, leaving a bag of groceries on our porch on her way home. She knew an avid hunter, and soon deer meat was also delivered to our door.

We prayed for furniture and beds to sleep in. God sent a Sunday school class who heard about our family's plight to our home with two trucks full of furniture they found in their own storage rooms and attics.

We prayed for a car. God gave us new friends who loaned vehicles and offered rides until one evening after our first American Thanksgiving dinner, the host handed over the keys to a new Toyota Previa van for our family to use for however long we needed it.

When my littlest sibling and sister, Libby, decided to finally make her grand entrance into the world, someone covered the obstetrician's fee anonymously. We never learned who it was. Utility bills and sometimes rent needs were met by "love offering" checks from local churches when I performed for their youth groups or services. Somewhat shy at the time, I would be nervous days before because it took a lot of courage to stand and sing in front of my peers and adults. In some ways, I was embarrassed. But God always used these performances and offerings and at times even nailed the amount our family needed almost to the dollar.

Neighbors, friends, fellow church members, and strangers saw our need through the eyes of Christ and let faith and compassion move them to action.

God showed us He heard us through the extravagant kindness of our community. Because Mum and Dad were brave enough to be vulnerable and honest about our needs as a family, we were truly seeing God answer our specific prayers with miracle after mind-blowing miracle. As a kid, this was remarkable. This was proof to me that God was real, powerful, and cared deeply for me and my family.

Since then, here's what I've come to know about miracles: they never lose their wow factor.

When we feel like we have plenty, we tend to rely less on God. We look at our provisions like a home, groceries, and our clothes as things we either earned or are entitled to have. But when we're in need, everything is a miracle. You miss nothing because you're counting on God for everything. We were taken so far out of the box of our family's "normal life," that I got to experience God in extraordinary ways as a teenager. I witnessed people step up to tangibly be our answer to prayer and that inspired me profoundly in my faith and ministry.

There's a line in *Unsung Hero* where a recording company executive says to the actors playing my father and me, "What does a fifteen-year-old have to say about God anyway?" In real life, this was never said to my face, but the general remark was relayed to Dad. The true answer to that is, "A lot." I had a powerful testimony to share because of those living-by-faith years. I had so much to say about God because He moved on my family's behalf. I watched Him provide for us in unexplainable ways. He opened doors for us that seemed locked shut. Through the struggle, He bound our family in a kinship that prepared us to stand strong as a unit in the years of ministry ahead.

St. James

From his trips when we lived in Australia and spending years in the music business, Dad was well connected in Nashville before we ever arrived. So, he reached out to many of the record labels about my music and I began to audition for them. One of the executives he called was Eddie DeGarmo, of the Christian rock band DeGarmo and Key, who had just started a record label, and asked him to come hear me sing at The People's Church in Franklin, Tennessee. I was told he may show up but never actually knew for certain he was there, so I performed and worshipped just like I would at any other church service.

In the large Baptist church's sanctuary, I sang a few songs for a couple hundred congregants from my first Australian album, *Refresh My Heart*. One of the songs I sang was called "Power of God." I had rehearsed a dramatic pointing to the sky (to God) in my practices with Dad. It was edgy and therefore slightly uncomfortable to perform. My music and "Power of God" moves must have been effective though, because afterwards Eddie's daughter, Shannon (who was/is my age and now a good friend), was at the worship service and gave her dad her approval. She saw my authenticity and, even as a teenager, really valued seeing a peer use their gifts to worship God.

Sure enough, there was another miracle. Eddie caught the vision of what this fifteen-year-old, curly headed, Jesus-loving Aussie girl with a song in her heart had to offer. I was young, but God had been readying me for this moment since I said "yes" to Him at Girls Brigade. Shortly after my performance, I signed my first development deal with Eddie's label, ForeFront Records.

I was shocked when ForeFront suggested quickly that I change my name. Authenticity and humility are greatly valued in Australian culture, so initially my response was a negative one. Changing my name felt pretentious. Some amount of anonymity can be a protection for an artist though, especially when the artist is a young girl. So, I slowly became more open to it. "Rebecca St. John" was the name Eddie first suggested, but that felt too random to me—if I was going to do this, I wanted a stage name that had personal significance.

I was very close to my grandmother, so I called her to see if she had any ideas for names that might work. She suggested "Beasley," her maiden name, and a few others. Then at the end of the call, she offered "James," after her husband, my dad's father, who had passed away not long after we got to the States. We didn't have the resources for Dad to be able to fly back to Australia for the funeral, and that broke all our hearts, especially Dad's. So when my grandmother suggested "James," it confirmed an idea we had been having across the world. We thought we could blend ForeFront's idea of "St. John" with my grandfather's name and it would be a way to honor him, while also feeling authentic to me. Thus, "Rebecca St. James" took the stage.

I prayed that God would use me in this new venture of doing music in the US. I asked Him to strengthen me in this call He had on my life because I often felt painfully aware of my weaknesses. In His grace, God allowed my awareness of lack to become my superpower as it made me rely on the Holy Spirit to provide. As I transformed the songs in my heart into albums, I often recalled a quote I once heard that "God doesn't call the qualified, He qualifies the called" because He was doing just that for me. God gave me a manager in my father, a homeschool teacher and cheerleader in my mum, vocalists, setup crew, merch and lighting directors in my brothers, and a bass guitarist in my cousin.

Being so young yet bold in my faith, I was authentic and relatable to student audiences. With the release of my *God* album, my Christian peers were able to listen to lyrics I had written that were worship oriented and prayer focused. Some combination of my willingness to be vulnerable and the support from my manager of a dad and incredible team at ForeFront allowed my music to be almost instantly embraced across the world. Over the years, I played at concerts and events in England, Sweden, Norway, Romania, and Russia along with many other places across Europe. I even had the unique opportunity to go back to Australia and play at my former elementary school in New South Wales and my high school in Queensland. As I traveled the globe, I would sing "Blessed Be Your Name" and the audiences would often start to sing it with me in their own language. As I witnessed the diverse body of Christ praise His name, I was humbled by the fact that God was allowing me to play a little part in raising up the great song God was declaring across the world.

One of my favorite performances of all time was in Holland in the late nineties at a televised youth evangelism conference with over 30,000 young adults in an Amsterdam arena. I was singing songs from my *God* album, and through the entire concert it was so evident that the Holy Spirit was moving in their lives. As I walked through the crowds, students reached out towards me. We'd lock hands and I felt an instant friendship and connection with the people of Holland. These travels and concerts were beyond what I could have ever thought of when I gave my gifts to God all those years before.

While I was greatly impacted everywhere I went, there was one trip that will forever hold a special place in my heart. Shortly after I turned twenty and released my Christmas album, one of the first ministries I was able to support with my music, Compassion International, invited me to India. Compassion is a child sponsorship and charity organization that empowers local churches around the world to care for children in poverty.[3] I had been supporting a child through their organization and they so graciously provided for me the opportunity to meet her. As I toured my sponsored child's humble, one-room home and saw the joy she and her community had despite their hardship, my perspective about the world shifted. It became evident that you didn't need much for God to do remarkable things through you. This message was echoed by the atmosphere of the country at the time. I arrived shortly after Mother Teresa, a huge hero of mine, had passed and everyone was in mourning because of her loss and the incredible impact she had made. Mother Teresa's legacy and traveling through India to meet my Compassion child taught me that if we simply give God what we have, He'll bless the rest.

As my ministry expanded, that's exactly what I did—I gave God all I had and He kept surprising me as He blessed it. Often, when I became overwhelmed by the speed in which things were taking off, I would reflect back to our "living by faith" season when I cleaned homes and cared for children. While there was a part of me that loved the immediate difference you could make cleaning and caretaking, I had felt a bit like Cinderella as I took care of tasks while day-dreaming about a different season. I sensed back then that I wasn't living the adventure I was created for, in ministry or in life with a family of my own. So, when I was traveling the world in music, I was very aware that though part of the mission of my life had been realized, my prince had not yet come. I found myself in those years often asking God for a husband.

Suddenly, it was as if I had been whisked into a grand tale about music and love, revealing my relational dreams to the world as my ministry intersected with the True Love Waits movement.

Chapter 5

REVIVAL

Cubbie

I had no idea that God was going to write a "Revival" chapter into the pages of my life. What I did know for certain was that He was up to something great when the immediate thought I had after I first set foot in Paarl, South Africa, was *This feels like home*. Paarl (meaning "pearl" in Afrikaans) is a town about forty-five minutes from Cape Town. It's the largest town in the Cape Winelands with lush, rolling hills, beautiful vineyards, towering granite mountains, and a sloping valley that leads out to a glimmering sea. While I had just touched down in a country so unlike my own, I truly felt like I belonged there more than I did in California at that time. I was no longer just a nineteen-year-old aspiring artist finding my way through a post–high school season of exploration. I had a purpose. I was on a mission.

Despite multiple college acceptance letters, I decided to press pause on my scholastic pursuits after high school to focus on my band at the time. I picked up a job working for a private residential contractor learning the ins and outs of home building, and most of my after-hours were spent in rehearsal or playing gigs. The little free time I had outside of work and the band was devoted to volunteering with various ministries including a junior high boys' group, college-aged worship team, and the youth group I had recently graduated from. It was with that youth group on a typical Sunday morning that I heard about a mission team bound for South Africa that eventually led to me living in the country.

With my newfound passion for Jesus and a natural bent toward exploration, I had a deep sense that mission work lay somewhere in my future. Maybe the Middle East. Possibly the jungles of South America. However, at the time, I associated South Africa more with an epic surf adventure than a mission trip. So, when a representative shared with the youth group about the opportunity, I casually stated, "Cool. I'd love to go to South Africa one day." Instead of interpreting this comment as a general sense of wonder about the country, he took me seriously. Next thing I knew, I found myself at a training meeting.

"Cubbie! You're here! We've heard so much about you," greeted one trip goer. "We're so excited you're going with us!" smiled another. I had nowhere near committed to this trip, yet everyone in the group was already acting like I was part of the team. The more I learned, the more intriguing the opportunity sounded; the trouble was that I wasn't convinced God wanted me to go. So, I continued to attend to the meetings out of a weird sense of obligation knowing that I held the ultimate trump card to bow out—I did not have the $3,000 that was required. And then came the day that the money was due ...

Hanging my head, I approached the woman keeping track of all the accounting to deliver the bad news. "I'm so sorry. I don't have the money. I don't think I can go on the trip." I was stunned when she replied, "What do you mean? Your account has been paid in full. I've already put a deposit down on your airfare." I stepped away in absolute shock. *Okay, God, I guess You really want me to go on the trip ... but what the heck?* It's not that I wasn't incredibly grateful, I just still lacked peace about the trip and now felt forced into it. I struggled with that sense of restlessness up until our final team gathering.

As we began our meeting in a simple time of worship led by a girl playing her acoustic guitar, I heard it again. The Voice. It was the Voice that had cut through my previous cloud of depression and confusion. "Cubbie, I want you to go on this trip and I want you to stay longer than two weeks." With those words came an overwhelming sense of peace, not just about the two-week trip, but also about the potential of staying long term.

As I slowly came back to reality, I was hit with the ramifications of what I had just heard. *Stay longer than two weeks?* I couldn't just up and leave. I had a job, ministry responsibilities, and (of course) there was the band. In my heart, I began to pray, "Lord, if that was really You, You're going to have to take care of these things. Ball is in Your court." True to character, He took care of it all in just three days.

Over the few days that followed, I had a series of interesting phone calls and conversations. The college ministry I was leading randomly (or not so randomly) had a guy move into town who played bass and was passionate about worship. A few volunteers joined the youth group I was helping lead. My boss hired a new superintendent who could cover the jobs I was working on. And in the eleventh hour, the morning we were leaving, I got a call from the lead singer of the band. "Hey man, wanna grab a burrito before you head out?" To which I replied, "Of course!" He was a man on a mission as we sat down to eat. "I'm just going to cut to the chase. I don't know why, but I feel like the Lord is calling me to lay down the band." I sighed with unbelievable relief.

All the dots connected, and I had never experienced anything like it. Little did I know, that was just the start of all the miracles I was about to witness. God took everything I was carrying and placed it into safe hands that could hold it all. I was free to fly out on my "two-week" mission trip across the world.

How quickly two weeks became two years.

Words, Visions, and Dreams

As I recount my time spent in South Africa, and then share into my adult life, you're going to hear me reference more prophetic words, visions, and dreams that I received. So, before we keep going, we need to break down why they are important.

In 1 Corinthians 14:1, Paul makes a compelling case for desiring the gift of prophecy and operating in it when he says, "Follow the way of love and eagerly desire gifts of the Spirit, especially prophecy." Depending on the kind of church you've grown up in, you may have seen the gifts of the Spirit play out in different ways. I grew up in a church that was by and large not super charismatic. Spiritual gifts were acknowledged but not necessarily pursued. So, my introduction to the prophetic was as a by-product of raw supernatural encounters with the Holy Spirit.

For instance, I received my first vision in the midst of worship as a teenager. I closed my eyes to focus my heart on the words I was expressing to my Creator and suddenly I started seeing incredibly vivid pictures. It was wild when I later saw the meaning behind them come to fruition in my life. This wasn't something I was chasing, felt like I needed, or even knew to develop. It was a natural thing that just evolved through being in the presence of the Holy Spirit. So, as I've gotten older and learned more about prophecy, here's what I've concluded:

Prophetic words, visions, or dreams can be used by God to communicate to His people in pivotal or poignant moments to direct or encourage. I've come to know when something is a word from the Lord when it aligns with God's Word, is affirmed by God-honoring counsel, and is accompanied by a peace that transcends understanding.

Someone once asked me, "How do I know if I'm really receiving a vision, prophetic word, or dream, and when did I just eat a bad burrito?" The answer is simple. Scripture against all other words is the ultimate test. Just ask: Is this word in alignment with Scripture? If it's not, it's not from the Lord. It's a bad burrito. If it aligns with God's Word, then hold on to it. A prophetic word will never supersede or replace the Word of God. Always test everything against Scripture and then see how God plays it out in your life.

It's important to add that, while God can speak to us at any time that He wants, we typically won't hear from Him daily in prophetic ways. There are often breaks or periods of prolonged silence. In these silent seasons we experience the most growth because we are forced to live on the faith that God is who He says He is and His Scripture is the only expression of capital T truth. In those times between words, visions, or dreams, the previous word God spoke can help guide and carry us through. We should enjoy the gaps, sitting in the silence, and not strive to contrive another prophetic word because there is a danger in desiring prophecy or encouragement over the Word of God. We can begin to think we need a constant word, vision, or dream to function rather than rely on God or simply walk under the authority of Scripture as we go about our daily lives.

A modern parable that breaks down the way God typically prophetically speaks to us goes like this:

> *There's a father and son. The father doesn't need to enter the room and tell the son what he's going to be doing that day. For the most part, the son knows what to do already. However, there are moments along the boy's growth journey where the father will need to come in and say, "Today we're going to have a change. You've been used to staying home and playing with your toys. But today you're going to leave your house and start kindergarten. It's going to be a new experience." As the boy starts kindergarten, the father guides him through his new routine. After*

the son figures it out, the father doesn't need to come in and say, "Today we're going to kindergarten ..." every single day. He really doesn't come back for another father-son talk until there's a change coming in the boy's direction. Eventually the dad will say, "Okay, Son. Today you're leaving kindergarten and starting first grade." There's a new teacher and classroom so the father walks him through this transition and offers him direction and guidance in the midst of change.

My own experiences with prophecy are very much in line with this story. The Lord has stepped in for me at pivotal moments of transition, forks in the road, or in seasons of disillusionment or discouragement. With extremely specific words for that moment in time, He's used dreams, visions, and prophetic words from fellow believers to offer me clarity on the direction I should move in for the next season or place.

God has been using the prophetic as a form of communication since the dawn of time to offer warnings, encouragement or hope, symbolism for the future, and to audibly speak or give direction (see Genesis 20, Genesis 28, Genesis 37, Matthew 1, 1 Kings 3 for a few examples). As far as our modern dreams go, I think Acts 2:17 still calls us to pay attention to them as well when it says, "In the last days, God says, I will pour out my Spirit on all people. Your sons and daughters will prophesy, your young men will see visions, your old men will dream dreams."

Generally speaking, many dreams are ludicrous. They are often wild and nonsensical, simply a compilation of the subconscious processing life. However, if a dream is really pressed on your heart and mind when you wake up, pay attention. There might be key images, components, or feelings that you may notice. Sit in the presence of the Holy Spirit as you process those feelings. Pray through it. He will be clear when there are dreams you need to regard.

We don't have to over-spiritualize prophecy, visions, and dreams because there's a simplicity to the way that God uses them for practical and pointed purposes—always for the building up of His people and the Church. We don't need to complicate this because true gifts of the Spirit will never supersede Scripture. While it's incredible to receive a prophetic word, we should never "need another word" because we have His Word to guide us every day.

In short, when it comes to the prophetic, move forward holding it all up to God and testing it under the authority of Scripture, and Godly counsel.

Okay, back to South Africa ...

Home

Just before I left, a friend shared with me a vision God gave them on my behalf. They told me, "I can see you swinging a hammer and building a house. This is going to be a place of hope, healing, and restoration." I shouldn't have been, but I was soon surprised to learn that one of the main projects with our church's partner organization, Miqlat (meaning "place of hope" or "refuge" in Hebrew[4]), was building an orphanage for children affected by AIDS. It felt like one of those "God wink" moments, especially when one of the Miqlat leaders announced to the group that they were searching for people skilled in the trades to help in the building process. I had just spent the previous year of my life learning home construction!

Over the next two weeks the team and I became well acquainted with the multiple arms of ministry Miqlat was busy with throughout the Paarl valley, with our main task being teaching life skills in the local public schools. When I wasn't with students, I was able to pick up a hammer and help build the orphanage. It did eventually become a place where babies were healed and abandoned children sought shelter. As each day passed, my fondness for that land and those people grew, making me feel increasingly at home.

The day before I was scheduled to head back to the States, I had to make the call to my parents. Deep sigh ... "You won't need to come to the airport tomorrow ... I'm not coming home," I told them as I held my breath. I thought they might be upset, but to my shock, they weren't even surprised. God had been preparing their hearts for me to stay the whole time. They too had a sense that I was where I was meant to be and needed to stay. Clearly, God is in *all* details.

Now a long-term missionary, Miqlat threw me into a full-time teaching position in a local Black school during the day, afterschool sports programs in the Coloured communities, a discipleship training program on the weekends, and the orphanage renovation project (in my spare time). Before you run out and try to get me "canceled," these were, and still are, the "politically correct" terms for the three major people groups in South Africa. Whites are typically descendants of British or Dutch colonists, who speak English or Afrikaans (a descendant language of Dutch). Blacks are those of pure tribal descent who speak native African languages. And Coloureds are a multiracial people group that have ancestry from both African and European people, who primarily speak Afrikaans.

Immediately apparent to anyone visiting or living in South Africa are the lingering effects of apartheid, an almost five-decade-long stretch of segregation that divided the country from the 1940s to early 1990s. During that time, the government went through every city, drew a line down the middle, and the Whites were given one side, and the Blacks and Coloureds were forced to live on the other. Whites had primary access to resources, education, and jobs during apartheid, and as a result their sides of the cities were beautifully built up to the standard of any first world nation, while the opposite sides of these cities were driven into utter poverty. It was an incredibly bizarre experience to traverse some of the most beautiful city streets, lined with incredible restaurants, coffee shops, shopping plazas, resorts, wineries, golf courses, and in an instant, cross some sort of arbitrary boundary and immediately find yourself in some of the worst third world living conditions you could imagine.

Over my time in Paarl, I learned that the spiritual complications of the cultural and physical boundaries ran incredibly deep. While people in all areas

I worked in were very aware of the spiritual word, there was a cultural confusion that plagued their identities and left many not knowing what to believe about themselves or their Creator. Apartheid had certainly succeeded in distorting a general perception of reality and spirituality.

Four years prior to this trip, at the worship conference where I encountered Jesus for the first time, I saw one of my first visions. Here's what I recall: *There was a town that was divided by a river in the middle of it. The river slowly creeped over its banks and eventually flooded the entire town. Yet, the flood was not destructive, rather it brought people together as it erased the boundary between them, and they all found themselves in the same unifying life-giving water.*

As I looked out at Paarl with its river being used as the former apartheid boundary line, I had a deep sense that this was the town God had shown me. And that meant the flood was coming.

Sing Again

Setting out to walk into town on a Saturday afternoon to meet up with some students at a coffee shop, I took a moment to stroll through a small garden near the town center. For someone who had been so restless at home, wondering what the future held, what my career would look like, who I would marry ... I was surprisingly at peace thousands of miles across the ocean. I paused, looked to the sky, and in that moment came to truly understand that there was nothing else I needed except Jesus. I didn't need to have life all figured out. God was with me, and He was holding me. I could feel it ... almost tangibly. I could hear Him as He gently whispered, "Okay, now you can start opening your mouth."

Shortly after the team of Americans returned home without me, I felt God ask me to simply close my mouth. It wasn't a reprimand, but a prompt to be still in His presence. To be silent and to just listen and learn, from Him and the people He had placed in my life. But now, from a place of full reliance, surrender, and contentment in Jesus, the prompt was to open my mouth. There was plenty that I was excited and ready to start sharing, but it seemed like God's call was to do more than just share ... *Was He leading me to sing again?*

The Dutch Reformed Church connected with our ministry in Paarl needed a worship leader. As the dude who showed up to South Africa with a backpack, guitar, and video camera, I was clearly "the artsy guy" and that made me a natural candidate. The only issue was that I did not lead worship, so I kept telling them "no." Please find somebody else. I hadn't freely "opened my mouth" in melody in over a decade since I lost my voice as a boy back in Bakersfield. However, now sensing that it was God asking me to, I felt responsible for saying "yes." After all these years, God wanted to perform a miracle for me. *Could God really give me my voice back?*

Trusting God would come through, I finally agreed to come lead worship at a Sunday evening youth service I had attended a handful of times prior to this particular evening. Each gathering there was just a small handful of kids (like two or three). So that night, I strapped on my acoustic guitar, stepped to center stage, and saw the couple of familiar faces awkwardly standing in the expansive, empty youth hall. As lifeless as the church was at the time, at least it felt like a safe spot to start singing. If something went wrong, I wouldn't be too embarrassed. The kids were already so disengaged that I didn't think they'd even notice. I opened my mouth, and ... like a friend, I felt the Holy Spirit say, "It's time. You've got this." And I did it. I sang.

The Flood

It was to this Dutch Reformed Church on the White side of town that I was sent by Miqlat, to not only lead worship, but help build a youth ministry. It was the most dead, unenthusiastic, and least likely place for a revival. That's probably why God started it there. The first Sunday that I showed up to help with their youth group, there was a guy onstage preaching at three kids in an auditorium. *Awesome.* By the bored, disinterested expressions on the kids' faces,

I could tell they clearly did not want to be there. Yup, I started in a negative space rather than at ground zero.

Building relationships as a teacher in the local schools taught me that my best move in this scenario, if we wanted to see a youth ministry form, was to just get to know the kids in their environment. So, I spent a ton of time after school where these affluent teenagers were hanging out at fancy coffee shops and restaurants. It quickly became evident to me that these kids struggled with what most of us in America battle against as well. Having our physical needs not only met, but overcompensated for, can often blind us to our spiritual needs. As I started building relationships and connecting with a core group of students in the community, I began extending invitations to the Sunday evening youth service. Over the next several weeks the attendance of that meager little youth group slowly began to grow.

I caught wind of a ministry that was coming to town to host a weekend retreat for students in the mountains. The core youth group and I did our best to get the word out, and to my surprise around sixty kids showed up outside of the Dutch Reformed Church to cram into a bus and trek up the mountain for camp. These were the cool kids, dropped off by parents driving BMWs and Mercedes, more likely to be found at the hippest weekend party, not volunteering to attend a Jesus retreat. I couldn't help but make the comparison to the similar irrational choice I had made years earlier to get into the fifteen-seater van that took me to a worship conference where I met Jesus and my life drastically changed. While it didn't make much logical sense, I was pleasantly amused by whatever God was up to.

We arrived in a setting that I can only liken to Rivendell from Lord of the Rings. We were surrounded by towering mountains, green grass, and flowing waterfalls. It was stunning. After playing a few pickup games of rugby and our first teaching session, we all showed back up in the recreation hall for a time of worship. I expected a typical camp musical moment where kids would sing, pray, and part ways. In the boys' dorm we'd all stay up way too late eating junk food, picking on each other and laughing about nothing funny. Instead, this moment of worship felt like what I had read about Pentecost. The Holy Spirit showed up so evidently that students were physically responding by falling on their faces and worshipping God.

These most unlikely of Christ converts were overwhelmed by the Holy Spirit and God they just met, as I had been in high school. They didn't want to stop worshipping and praying for each other. When we finally had to wrap up the weekend and head back down the mountain, there was a natural excitement to reconvene at church the following Sunday. We went from a small, partially engaged group to sixty-plus radically repentant, miraculously saved, passionate Jesus followers. That sixty-plus quickly grew to hundreds. Students kept coming and inviting their friends week after week, and we eventually ran out of room. Our church became an initial landing place for whatever God was doing amongst the youth of Paarl, and we witnessed a full-blown revival.

The beautiful thing was that the revival didn't stay confined to the youth. It spread like a fire into the main congregation of the church, and eventually to neighboring churches, communities, towns, and beyond. There were too many kids for me to be supporting this movement alone, so I appointed student leaders, helped them organize small groups, and put together a worship team. Fairly quickly these youth who were completely sold out for Jesus began leading their own Bible studies and worship gatherings on their school campuses, in their homes, and throughout the community.

With revival underway, a big part of my push over the next year and a half was reconciliation—to destroy the dividing lines and bring students of different races who were living in the same town together. With the Miqlat youth team, I began creating events that would draw in kids from the other side of the river. As the Holy Spirit seemed to continue moving throughout the city, our church hosted a couple of worship nights where buses of Coloured and Black kids traveled to the White side of town and vice versa. For the first time, White teenagers who grew up in neighborhoods full of fancy houses and shiny cars were seeing what life looked like on the other side of the river. At these events, God's presence would stir compassion in these teens for their brothers and sisters of all races. The student revival continued to explode as they began to form their own united church community, linked together by their newfound identity in Jesus.

The vision came to pass. The flood of the Holy Spirit overwhelmed the river and brought the people together. Praise God.

Phone Call to the Future

There are countless stories from my season in South Africa, but if I could sum up my two years, I would say it was a deep dive into learning who Jesus is and the breadth of ways that God can move. He can miraculously heal, unite people in impossible circumstances, start a full-blown revival with just a spark of faith, and celebrate the worship of His people from the remote bush of Namibia to the megachurches in massive cities like Cape Town. I learned the supernatural power that exists when you cross cultural lines in the name, and with the love and peace, of Jesus. So much of who I am today is a direct result of my season in South Africa, and the ways in which I saw and experienced the power of our incredible God.

There was nothing better than being in the middle of where God was moving. As far as I was concerned, I was going to spend the rest of my life in South Africa. I had fallen in love with the country and the people. I had built some of the closest relationships that I had ever experienced and had even started dating an incredible girl. With that relationship being so centered on Jesus, it was definitely looking like marriage material. So at the point that the organizations our team had built were looking like they could run without me at the helm, I began to look for the next thing I was to put my hand to.

The crazy thing was, every opportunity I explored with other ministry partners, nonprofits, and even universities seemed to be a closed door. My sense of peace in South Africa slowly began to disappear. With my visa running out, I needed to get some answers quickly. *Where was God leading me next?* I was devastated by the thought of leaving this beautiful place that had given my heart and soul a home. Everything seemed so right, yet at the same time I could feel God beginning to point me in a different direction. Though it broke my heart, I knew at that point my days in South Africa were numbered.

Per usual, our ministry team was dragging ourselves out of bed at four-thirty in the morning for our daily worship and prayer time. The fluorescent lights were abruptly switched on and startled the entire meeting room into wakefulness. I rubbed my eyes, grabbed my guitar, and started strumming something either by Matt Redman, Martin Smith, or Tim Hughes (my go-to worship leaders at the time). With my eyes closed, I started singing and the staff followed me into worship.

That's when I had a vision. At first it wasn't clear, but then it was like God started to draw me into a bird's-eye view overlooking a mall in Newport Beach, California, called Fashion Island. I saw the mall with its big open courtyard, grassy knolls, and babbling fountains. The birds were chirping, and I could feel the breeze on my face as the warm summer sun was setting serenely over the Pacific Ocean. God then yanked me up above the clouds to see in the distance a view of Vanguard University, a school I had been to several times with my youth group for Soul Survivor worship conferences. Those conferences had always left a powerful and life-changing impression on my heart. While in the area, we would visit Fashion Island and enjoy a picnic in the grass. I had applied and was accepted to Vanguard before graduating high school. It was never high on my list of schools I had thought about attending, but something in this vision sparked my curiosity.

It soon became abundantly clear the purpose of this vision was Vanguard. It was there that God was calling me to go. College was the next thing to put my hand to.

"We still have your application on file. We even have an open spot for you next semester if you'd like it," the admissions officer informed me when I finally worked up the courage to call. There was not only a dorm room open for me, but there were scholarships still attached to my application. And because of my high school AP credits, I could also walk back into school with a whole semester's worth of class hours under my belt. In the wake of countless closed doors, this one was undeniably wide open, and it was time to walk through.

The hardest part wasn't that phone call into the future, it was telling my South African team and friends who had become my family that I was leaving. We had a series of braais (proper South African BBQs) and surf trips to commemorate our time together. I set up replacements for my jobs at all our ministries. I was hopeful for the future yet heartbroken at the same time. These people and this country had taught and inspired me so much.

Part of that inspiration was found while capturing people's stories on the small video camera I brought with me. As a result, I made the decision to study film production and anthropology with the intention to bring that education back to the mission field. I would make documentaries and give voice to God's children across the world by telling their stories. Through film, South Africa inspired me to want to raise awareness and rally churches to support causes that may otherwise go unknown.

I had rediscovered my voice. Now it was my turn to learn how to give others a platform and tell them that God hears them too.

Vanguard

I spent about a month (including Christmas and New Year's) with my family when I came back to California. Most nights, I tossed and turned as I struggled my way through the reentry process. I didn't want to be back in the States. My internal compass felt broken. My heart hurt from losing the country and people I loved. Everything ached. I seriously questioned if I had made the right decision to leave. Things went on like that until I drove my small Toyota truck with what little clothing I was still carrying in my backpack, guitar case, and camera up to The Towers at Vanguard. With their white cinder block walls and tiny windows, my new home was more prison-like than dorm-like. *Great, God sent me to jail.*

"Do you have anything else?" the resident assistant asked me as I unloaded my truck and started to head up to my room on the third floor. He looked confused as I shrugged, "Nope, that's it" and began climbing the stairs.

After getting the grand tour of my new "home" and meeting a group of guys on my dorm floor, I eventually retreated to my room to try to settle in. That night, to my utter surprise, I had the most peaceful and restful night of sleep that I had ever experienced. I woke the following morning in the presence of an overwhelming peace that surpassed any understanding. It was that peace that served as the indicator that I was exactly where God wanted me. And with that I was able to fully give myself to this new chapter God was writing in my life. Holding both joy and sadness, I began classes confident Vanguard was exactly where I needed to be.

I was ready now to tell stories through film but had no clue how my own life would play out.

Chapter 6

TRUE LOVE WAITS

Rebecca

Teen: "Why do you want to be a nun?"
Nun: "Because I want to help people."
Teen: "So why don't you just become a nurse? You could help people and still have sex."

Everything was fine in my audition for *Sister Act 2* until I read the last line. I knew that it was all pretend, that I was simply being asked to bring to life a character with a personality, perspective, and moral code unlike my own. This is part of acting—and even the intrigue of it. But the script felt so incongruent with my own convictions that I couldn't deliver the line convincingly. Perhaps I never thought about it directly until that moment, but even as a fifteen-year-old, I passionately believed that sex was a sacred gift from God, something meant only to be enjoyed with a spouse. And I couldn't be brought to mock it even if it was for a fictional scene in a movie I really wanted a role in.

Though I did make it through the first round of auditions, I didn't make the cut for the cast of *Sister Act 2*. Thank God I didn't make jokes about sex in a movie. Shortly after, I was asked by organizers of True Love Waits rallies to sing and say a few words about the importance of honoring God in our relationships and with our bodies. True Love Waits was a campaign that launched in the '90s across the US promoting a biblically based charge for teens to remain sexually abstinent until marriage.

When I think of the word *purity*, one of the first things that comes to mind is the scripture "Blessed are the pure in heart, for they will see God" (Matt. 5:8). When we seek purity of heart, in all aspects of our lives, we have greater ability to see God. What a motivating idea!

I was exposed to these concepts about abstinence growing up because there was always an open door to conversations about sexuality in my home. Between talking about it with my parents, solid teaching at church, and a sense of rightness in my spirit, I landed on the personal conviction that sex was an incredibly good but holy thing that God designed to be shared in the intimacy of a marriage.

So, when I was asked to speak in front of local churches, schools, rallies, or even 60,000-plus people in the Georgia Dome at the True Love Waits: Through the Roof event in 1996, it all felt very natural and authentic. Purity was a choice I had made, so this was a space I was already committed to live in, privately and publicly. At that event, where I was both hosting and singing, 340,000 pledge cards from around the world were stacked from the floor to the roof of the stadium. The pledge cards read "Believing that true love waits, I make a commitment to God, myself, my family, my friends, my future mate, and my future children to a lifetime of purity, including sexual abstinence from this day until the day I enter a biblical marriage relationship."

I was a virgin and was committed to being one until I got married. Though slightly awkward in certain moments because this message was so countercultural, I was very much at peace with talking about it, because this support for young people committed to purity was much needed. From one teen to another, I could let my peers know they were not alone in this decision to live their lives God's way, the way the Bible encourages us to live.

More than anything, I felt led to be an encouragement to my generation, to love God in *all* areas of life. I always knew that sin, in its variety of forms, was sin. Pride, wrongdoing, breaking a commandment, and impurity ... anything against the heart of God forms a cloud between us and Him, between us and others. We all make these mistakes and find ourselves distant from God and the people we love. That's why, through Jesus, there's forgiveness and abounding grace.

Often in my shows, I would talk about the forgiveness available to all of us and the concept of a "second virginity." We can all always start over with God and decide to make the decision for purity even if we had already made mistakes or chosen to have sex before marriage. I didn't want anyone getting caught in that shame trap, because in Christ "there is no condemnation" (Rom. 8:1).

The point of this movement for me was freedom. Freedom within the good boundaries that God created for us in the Bible. When we read verses like 1 Thessalonians 4:3–4, which says, "It is God's will that you should be sanctified: that you should avoid sexual immorality; that each of you should learn to control your own body in a way that is holy and honorable," I believe God is saying, "Child, come and enjoy the world I have created for you, in freedom, without being controlled by the flesh. Thrive in joy as you walk in the Way that I have designed you to live."

Even speaking in the most awkward of spaces, like high schools or in Europe, where I thought this message wouldn't be received well, I always got a resounding "thank you" and applause in response. Teens would come up to me afterwards and say, "I'm so grateful to know that I'm not alone in this." Parents would often shake my hand with grateful tears in their eyes.

When Josh Harris came to me and asked me to write the foreword for his book *I Kissed Dating Goodbye*, my answer was an easy "yes." Josh had interviewed me for his homeschool magazine *New Attitude* and we became quick friends. He'd come to see me at concerts when I was near where he lived in Oregon, and we'd bump into each other at events.

I found his book encouraging in the way it talked about how dating was a mature commitment. Getting to know someone for the future purpose of marriage is where the rubber meets the road, and we must decide if we are going to honor God's Word about purity and steward well the heart of the person we're in a relationship with. Will we choose to not create any sin barriers between us and God, or us and others in the process of courting? We don't have to chuck dating out the window, but we need to be doing this well. We need to contemplate the weight of having a boyfriend or girlfriend, not treat people like they're disposable after a season. Love God. Love others. Let's not treat dating like most of culture does, let's look at it through a loving, biblical lens. I could totally get behind a message like that, so I did.

I didn't anticipate the danger of the True Love Waits or I Kissed Dating Goodbye movements. I don't think the people who created them did either. Intentions were so good, there's no way anyone knew there would be groups of people and churches who would take this message so literally and oversimplify it. It wasn't fathomable that they would turn this movement into a set of rules that promoted fear and legalism, rather than promoting that our purity and dating life should be led by the Holy Spirit.

Even recently, a friend told me how during this time her church full of college students decided to not date altogether. They "kissed dating goodbye" as if it wasn't needed at all. I think they (and many others too) see now that these teachings were taken to extremes and often led to many unspoken and sometimes even spoken rules. *Don't date, it's bad. Sex ... it's bad.* This was damaging stuff, and I hurt for those whose hearts and souls were wounded during that time.

The flip side of this messaging is that both of these things, dating (or "courting" as we often called it at that time) and sex are good, really good! I believe that when handled in a God-honoring way, these are very beautiful gifts from God. However, fear was often perpetuated around these topics in the nineties and early two thousands, when faith-building was the intent. So many teens were, at the time, terrified to do the wrong thing when God just wanted us all to take steps in the right direction toward honoring Him and our future spouse.

On the flip side, I have many friends who were encouraged and blessed by the True Love Waits movement, as Cubbie and I were. The same goes for countless concert goers I have met who have told me and continue to tell me how much those messages gave them strength to wait for the person God had for them.

While many of the young adults in my generation were making decisions about what they thought about purity, I continued praying for the spouse I believed one day I wouldn't have to wait for any longer. While my music career continued to climb, my "courting" life became more difficult and disappointing. True love did wait when it came to finding my future husband one day. Little did I know how long, painful, and lonely that wait would be for me ...

Cubbie

Prior to my time in South Africa, I had set my sights on Los Angeles. It was midway through high school when I switched my focus from baseball to music and film and concluded that LA was where I needed to be. It was in that season that I upgraded from my old Memphis guitar to that beautiful, sea-foam blue, 1950s-vibe Fender Stratocaster of my dreams. (I still have it, by the way.) In that season, I also became obsessed with shooting photography, which spiraled into an obsession with telling stories through film.

When I moved to South Africa, I valued my guitar and video camera more than clothes, so they were the most valuable things I packed. I may not have had a ton of outfits to choose from, but I got to gather tons of beautiful songs, stories, and images from my time serving in Paarl. So when God brought me to Vanguard, I chose to pursue a degree in communication with an emphasis in film production. I minored in anthropology and biblical studies, all with the intent of heading back to the mission field to make documentaries.

Halfway through college, I fell in love with the art of storytelling through scripted narrative, which shifted my sights back to LA. This was my focus as I worked my way through my final two years at Vanguard, but with graduation rapidly approaching and the smell of freedom becoming more palpable, I began to second-guess my plan. I was about to be free to do absolutely anything I wanted. There were no more classes to attend, no more papers to write, and there was no one telling me I had to move to LA. I could move back to South Africa if I wanted to. *Hmm* ... After a fair amount of debating and wrestling with God, He made it clear that LA was indeed my next destination.

So I graduated and off I went to move into an apartment with my friends and former college roommate right in the heart of historic Hollywood. We were walking distance from the Walk of Fame and my gym was next to the iconic Grauman's Chinese Theatre. It doesn't really get much more "LA" than that.

The day I got the key to my apartment and sat down on the living room sofa after unpacking my small handful of belongings, I should have felt excited to start setting off toward the pursuit of a career in the land of artists and dreamers. But I didn't. I was restless and missing South Africa, my ex-girlfriend, and still not completely content with the result of my last wrestling match with God. Finally, I couldn't sit still and wallow in my frustration and homesickness for a faraway country any longer. So, I hopped up to go to the place I always found peace and direction—the great outdoors.

There was a famous trailhead within walking distance from our apartment that ascended a portion of the Hollywood hills. It offered incredible views of the iconic Hollywood sign, the Griffith Observatory, and the entire city of Los Angeles. It was a rare, clear day where the city smog wasn't covering the horizon, so when I crested the peak of the trail and turned around, I could see all LA laid bare before me. God and I had been soul-wrestling as I trudged up the dusty trail. I laid out for Him everything I was feeling. I gave Him every doubt and fear. Then, as I stared at the city filled with skyscrapers, record labels, film studios, and a countless sea of dreamers, I could feel God tell me in that remarkably familiar, near-audible voice, *"This is your new mission field."*

From that moment on, my purpose for being in LA was restored. Like South Africa, I decided I could again build something! So, I did. I immediately used all my connections from school to plug into film and TV productions, jumped on staff at a local church, and joined a Bible study full of guys who were also artists. And while I thought my sole purpose for being there was film, shortly after this experience, I had a dream that proved to shed light on another avenue I was meant to explore.

In the early morning, I was awakened (in my dream) by my phone ringing. "Hello?" "Hey Cubbie, this is Jeff Tweedy." Jeff Tweedy is the lead singer of one of my favorite bands, Wilco. "Dude, we're in town. I know you live right up the street, can you meet me for coffee? There's something I want to talk to you about." *Sure, Jeff... Tweedy.* I hung up the phone, got dressed, walked down to the coffee shop, and sat down with Jeff.

"Hey man, we're on your tour right now and our bass player is going on hiatus. Would you be open to joining the band?" he stated. "Man, I just moved to LA to pursue film." I was now confused because Jeff and Wilco meant a ton to me. I didn't come here to do music, right? "Let me think about it," I replied as I rushed off to gain some insight from my roommates. I bust in the door and tell them everything. "You have to do this!" they declared. Then I woke up.

At face value, I know this just seems like a crazy dream. But I felt God asking me to pay attention to it. As I prayed through the elements of the dream, God reminded me of the multiple words of prophecy He had spoken over my life in regards to music. It was like He didn't want me to forget about music completely while I was there in LA. It was clearly something I was still deeply passionate about. While I had played bass for several years at that point, I felt prompted to really hone my craft as a player. So I found a bass instructor and began to spend every free moment I had practicing. Interestingly enough, one of the first guys I met after moving to LA was a guy named Mark Foster.

Foster the People

Mark is truly a fascinating individual with a radical story of his own. We met through a group of aspiring Christian actors, writers, and musicians. It did not take long to discover that he was, and still is, hands down a musical genius. We had slowly developed a friendship over the course of my first few years in LA, and connected over a common desire to use art as a vehicle to bring Truth to the world. We talked about getting together to make music several times over those few years, but for various reasons, it never worked out.

Finally, the time came and we were going to make it happen. Foster's previous project hadn't come together in the way he had hoped, and he was intent on finding a group of guys to start something new with. He introduced me to his friend and drummer, also named Mark (Pontius), and we put a day on the calendar to get together to just jam.

We met at Pontius' studio/apartment, which was in the heart of Hollywood. It was more of a bunker than a studio that was accessed through a nondescript door at the end of a pretty sketchy alleyway. There were no windows, and musical equipment encompassed the walls, floor, and a small studio desk.

Somewhere within the thrill of the first handful of chords and rhythms we played together, we could sense we had something incredibly special and quite unique between us. By the time that session concluded, the ringing in our ears seemed to match the ringing in our heart to chase whatever had just developed in that room. The band quickly became our passion project that we initially called "Foster and the People." When people repeatedly misheard it as "Foster the People," we realized that name was more in line with the heart of the project, so we set it in stone. We devoted all our odd hours between jobs to rehearsing. Foster used his connections to start booking us shows around town and eventually up and down the West Coast. We slowly began to build a small following, and then Foster showed us a song he had worked up called "Pumped Up Kicks," which would prove to change everything.

Knowing there was something special about that song, we started playing it live and began giving it away on our website in exchange for an email address. With all the conversions, and no simple automation at the time, we'd sit for hours on end typing in emails and personally sending responses back with an mp3 of the song. One day, a well-known fashion designer, Anna Sui, reached out to ask us if she could use our song in her review video of LA fashion week. *I mean sure.* In a time when "viral" was not necessarily associated with a lot of views, the video did seem to go viral as a result of people trying to figure out what the song was. What felt like overnight, a pretty serious buzz about the band was born.

As a result, we landed on an internet top 100 list called Hype Machine. It was a website that the music industry watched intently to see what was resonating with music listeners online. Over the next couple weeks after Anna's review was posted, "Pumped Up Kicks" kept climbing its way up the chart. We all completely lost it when it cracked into the top ten. We were in complete disbelief when it made it into the top three. And our brains practically fell out of our heads when it hit #1.

Days after the song made it to #1, *NME* (*New Musical Express*) magazine out of the UK published an article on us. All of a sudden (while I was still starving), I wasn't just a starving artist, but I was an artist in a band being talked about by magazines, websites, and radio stations that I had revered. We were quickly becoming known by the world, and we sensed that our lives were about to change in a major way.

HEAR MY PRAYER

Rebecca

After a few years in the True Love Waits movement, singing my songs and speaking across the nation about purity, I got a message from a friend saying, "Purity is such a huge topic for you. I think you should write a song about it." Right away, the wheels started turning in my head.

As I climbed into my bunk on my tour bus at the Creation Festival in George, Washington, I pulled out my journal and began to write, "Darling did you know that I dream about you, Waiting for the look in your eyes, When we meet for the first time ..." I was in a creative zone and something rare occurred. I wrote an entire song—lyrics, melody, and everything—in just one sitting. With the great and loving marriage of my parents as an inspiration, I dreamed of a spouse who would one day be mine, to have and to hold, and to partner with in everything. I'd always had a front row seat to their beautiful friendship and the love they shared. The lyrics to this new song organically flowed out of me and was just as easy to record when I arrived home in Nashville. The beat. The modern twist. This song was something special, I could feel it.

That's why when "Wait for Me" took off with my audience, I wasn't too surprised. I am a hopeless romantic. I love movies like *The Wedding Planner*, *While You Were Sleeping*, and *Pride and Prejudice*. This song engaged that part of my heart that believed in fairy tales coming true. However, I didn't predict how taxing it would be to sing, year after year, about a guy who may or may not exist. I ended up feeling increasingly vulnerable and exposed. Fears would play on my mind ... *Am I waiting in vain? What if my prince never comes?*

As the years went on and I kept singing "Wait for Me" at all my performances, I began to see that the Bible verse "hope deferred makes the heart sick" is true (Prov. 13:12). I longed for a spouse, but it seemed my schedule wouldn't allow me to meet him. I was moving out of my late twenties and into my thirties sad and exhausted by the knowledge that I didn't have a family of my own like I thought I would by now. But still I prayed that God would hear my prayer for a husband. I would keep singing ...

Darling did you know that I
I dream about you
Waiting for the look in your eyes
When we meet for the first time
Darling did you know that I
I pray about you
Praying that you will hold on
Keep your loving eyes only for me

I am waiting for
Praying for you, darling
Wait for me too
Wait for me, as I wait for you
Darling, wait

Darling did you know I dream about life together
Knowing it will be forever
I'll be yours and you'll be mine
And darling when I say
'Til death do us part
I'll mean it with all of my heart
Now and always, faithful to you

Now I know you may have made mistakes
But there's forgiveness and a second chance
So wait for me darling
Wait for me
Wait for me[5]

When we're asking God for anything, especially for the longings of our hearts for a spouse and a family, the hardest response for us modern Christians who live in a microwave culture to hear is, "Wait." When we're stuck in seasons of waiting, we start to wonder if God really hears us. Waiting for a baby, waiting for a dream to come true, a relationship to change, a job, our hearts to heal. Waiting is often tremendously hard. Or like me, when we're still single past the point on our own personal timeline that we thought we'd be married with children, we can question if Jesus really cares. *How do we know if God even hears our prayers when we, year after year, don't yet see them fulfilled?*

Here's what my season of being single and waiting on a spouse taught me—**God always hears.** First John 5:14–15 says, "And this is the confidence that we have toward him, that if we ask anything according to his will he hears us. And if we know that he hears us in whatever we ask, we know that we have the requests that we have asked of him" (ESV). God is not deaf.

He's not closing His ears or heart toward us when He pauses in response to our relationship requests. We just don't like asking for something we want and hearing God say "wait." Because it's at that moment we realize we may possibly be longing for what Jesus has to offer us more than we desire Jesus Himself. We can easily fall into wanting the blessing more than the Blesser of all things, a spouse more than the true Lover of our Souls, and children more than the presence of our Father.

If we think anything or anyone will complete us, we're going to be disappointed every time. We're not content in Jesus so we're most likely going to reach for wholeness and stability through physical or emotional connection. I'm sure I bought into the idea, even subconsciously that *"Oh, once I get married, I'm going to be so happy. My loneliness and insecurity will be gone."* Wise friends told both Cubbie and me, "If you can't find contentment before marriage, you're not going to find it post marriage." Boy is that true. If you're not content without a spouse, you'll be disappointed to find that marriage and sex, while both incredible blessings, do not fulfill or complete you. The challenge we must rise to as individuals is to seek contentment in God, find purpose in Christian community, and make peace with ourselves.

During this time of waiting, praying, and pursuing sexual purity, Philippians 4:12–13 came to life for us both. In these verses the apostle Paul writes, "I know what it is to be in need and I know what it is to have plenty. I have learned the secret of being content in any and every situation, whether well fed or hungry, whether living in plenty or in want. I can do everything through him who gives me strength." Paul discovered how to be content in the struggle, so he was also content when a particular struggle was over. Whether singleness is incredibly hard, or we love being on our own, **if we don't find contentment in Jesus in every season, we're not going to magically discover it when we get married.**

So, if the desire of your heart is to be married, and you have prayed so long for this that you doubt God even hears you, may I encourage you with the fact that He does in fact hear. He is so tender towards your longing that He offers Himself as enough while you wait. There is work only He can do in your heart in this season. True love does not ever have to wait with Jesus. So let yourself be loved perfectly by God as you wait well for a spouse. Don't lose heart or give up!

Knowing what I know now, my approach to purity is this: We do not need to look for a relationship to do the work that only Christ can. When we find out how to be content with the Blesser, we do not need to get something from someone to feel whole. Instead, we are able to see and receive our blessings in all our relationships with wide-open hands. **Waiting for sex within marriage isn't just a delay of gratification, it's a practice of faithfulness that carries over and blesses all seasons of life, especially marriage.**

I look back now and I see the things God was teaching me in the wait, and how He was moving my life forward, though at the time I felt stuck. God saw me struggling with my voice and He offered me an opportunity to begin to heal. He had given me a new life in California. Dreams had come true with my acting. My hope was restored, and I felt in that season that God would give me the strength to stay faithful in relationship to Him "even if" this dream of a spouse, one of the greatest longings of my heart, never came true.

We simply don't always get what we want when we want it. Sometimes we don't get what we most desire. Often, we have to do hard things. **But God always hears our prayers and answers with His comfort and presence. He is faithful to always be more than we need.** In my song "I Can Trust You," I wrote lyrics that are true for us all. "God, it hurts to give You what I must lay down. But when I let go, freedom is found. God it hurts to give You what I've held so dear, but because of Your love it's clear, I can trust You with this. I can trust You with me. I can trust You."[6]

In our seasons of trusting God with our desires for a spouse, here are a few tips Cubbie and I discovered on how to wait well:

1. Have fun and keep a close community.

Waiting doesn't have to be boring. And you don't have to be lonely in this season. The last few years of my singleness were rich in friendship, and they were fun! While we're longing for a spouse, we aren't princesses locked in a tower or princes combing the countryside for our long-awaited love. We are sisters, brothers, friends, coworkers, leaders … and a myriad of other things. Our identity and capability to love others well extends way beyond what we can offer a future spouse, so lean into all your other relationships. Go on adventures, grab coffee, travel. If you have a heart for children, find friends whose kids you can help care for. Identify married couples you would one day like to see your own future relationship reflect and get to know them. Ask them questions, learn, and grow. Life isn't on hold. Seize every moment of the single journey and enjoy it!

2. Get out of your comfort zone.

It is easy in a time of singleness to play it safe and stick "close to home." Perhaps it's insecurity or fear that makes us want to do this … I know I felt all these things in my dating years. But some of my best choices during that time were going to a "singles night" at a local church that I thought would be super awkward (it wasn't) and a Christian swing dancing event I regularly attended. I also journeyed to L'Abri in Switzerland (Francis Schaeffer's study center in the Swiss Alps) for two months during a sabbatical and it was life changing! A spontaneous "yes" to attending a party with my friends led me to meeting Cubbie (more on that soon). So, step out because you never know who you'll meet, what you'll learn, or how God will grow you in that space outside your comfort zone.

3. Have healthy dating boundaries.

Physical and emotional boundaries protect the hearts and bodies of both people in dating relationships. If we want to commit to upholding biblical standards like reserving sex for marriage, guarding our hearts, loving God, and treating others how we would want to be treated, we have to keep ourselves out of compromising situations. If we toe the line, all it takes is a good shove to push us over. So, decide early in your relationships to live above reproach!

When I had a significant other over, I made sure roommates were in the next room and the door propped open a little. Clothing could not be removed. These personal rules may sound conservative to some, but they were mutually agreed upon in my relationships and helpful in maintaining purity, not out of legalism, but out of relationship with God and a desire to honor Him. Discuss your boundaries with your significant other and be clear. Upholding biblical boundaries for dating sets you free to enjoy physical and emotional closeness, while setting you up for success in marriage. Cubbie and I can vouch for that.

4. Grow your relationship with Jesus.

Trust God's heart for you as you wait and grow in your intimacy with Him. A man or woman who has a deep love relationship with Jesus is extra attractive to the person who also has a strong and vibrant faith. In 1 Corinthians 7:33–34, Paul reminds us that when we are married, our attention is divided. When we're single, we have an ability to focus on connecting with Jesus in a way that is a bit harder to achieve in marriage and can become especially challenging when you have children. So, seize the opportunity to draw near to the one who has plans to "prosper you, not to harm you, to give you a hope and a future" (Jer. 29:11).

Wait well and do not "become weary in doing good" by laying down the timing of your life at Jesus' feet (Gal. 6:9). What Cubbie and I both want you to walk away with is the knowledge that God hears you and loves you perfectly. If you choose now to remain faithful to God's Word and Way, trusting His timing for your life, it will honor your spouse before you ever meet them and build lifelong trust in Jesus as you discover He truly completes you.

Cubbie

With all the incredible life movement and fulfillment of dreams surrounding the momentum with the band, there was a longing in my heart to share the excitement with a special someone. Like Rebecca, it had long been a desire of my heart to have a family. Growing up I was certain that I would be married by the time I was twenty-three, twenty-four at the latest, yet the timeline of my life wasn't panning out like I had thought it would. I was rapidly approaching twenty-eight at that point. While my past relationship had heartbreakingly ended, my time in South Africa had taught me that a Godly relationship with a Jesus-loving woman was possible. I couldn't shake wanting a connection like that again.

However, finding a Godly woman in LA that even came close to that bar was proving to become more and more unrealistic. The principles of Christianity were about as countercultural as it gets in the city, so to say you're truly a follower of Jesus took boldness. As a result of direct opposition, I watched as some "Christians" would maintain a love for Jesus while becoming lackadaisical in upholding all that He has asked us to do (or not do). At the time, we referred to this as "LA Theology," which unfortunately now has become all too prevalent throughout modern Christendom. Whether the excuse is that the Bible is outdated, or that the authors of the Scriptures didn't understand the pressures of social media, the areas of compromise generally fall around the conversation and practices surrounding sex.

While I know some people were turned off by legalistic interpretations of the True Love Waits movement, the virtues it upheld were biblical. The movement

was centered on encouraging young people to hold fast to the God-designed purpose for sex, a fierce desire to protect God's children, and hold His perfect design
for family as sacred. There were a lot of leaders and congregations that got this
right and encouraged students in the process, but there were also poor applica-
tions of this message that hurt people too. The sad reality is that, out of fear of
potentially offending or being accused of legalism, the fierceness to protect and
remind people of God's call to sexual purity seems to have subsided altogether.

I am grateful that my youth leaders did an excellent job navigating the
True Love Waits conversation and that it all had a positive impact on me. They
showed us the truth about sex in Scripture: it is a bonding agent in a marriage;
sex is good (so good in fact, God designed it as a gift you give to your spouse);
and being abstinent honors your future partner's heart and body. This all made
total sense to me from an early age, and the principles upheld and fought for
through the True Love Waits era resonated on a deep level. I was encouraged
and empowered by the champions of the movement to continue to stand on
those principles. I knew that being intimate needed to wait for the right person
and within the covenant of marriage. But this was completely counterculture
to the rock 'n' roll lifestyle I began to find myself face-to-face with every day.

There was a certain alluring ring to the LA Theology ... *Everybody is having
sex, there's forgiveness, it's okay!* It was not okay. I had committed long ago to
do this God's way, and I'd made it that far. I knew I couldn't give in, but then
sometimes it seemed like it would just be easier to throw in the towel and give
up my dream of finding that Godly woman. Was a marriage and family not
built on God better than no marriage or family at all? Maybe I could just keep
my mullet and mustache to ward off all the women. I'd be a hermit musician
and filmmaker for the rest of my life. Sounded very "LA" to me.

Listen, if you're wanting to give up on finding a Godly relationship because
He hasn't answered your prayers for a spouse yet, I get it. While I had the hope that
one could exist for me because I had a past relationship that was centered on Jesus,

maybe you haven't. You've been the only one pursuing God throughout your dating years. Or possibly you've been laying low when it comes to meeting other singles because having a relationship based on Godly principles just seems impossible. You too would have liked to join me in my dreams of being an artsy LA hermit.

The bar God sets for our relationships is high, and while it would be easy to limbo underneath and settle, please don't. Keep walking the narrow way and notice who happens to be headed down the same path. Those are the people who are set on Jesus. Their faith and growth are genuine and they're not going to need a future spouse to pull them in the right direction. They're already running toward God, so get to know them as you journey together.

While we should always hold to biblical standards, we can't idealize a dream version of a spouse and then quit dating because we're disappointed that people aren't perfect. This is what I was fearful that I was doing. Had I just concocted an image of the dream woman in my mind that was never actually going to appear in reality? But, as I prayed, I stayed openhanded about the "dream list" of what I hoped my wife would look like or do but remained tight fisted on what I knew God desired for me to pursue—a woman whose heart was set on Him. The challenging thing about modern dating is that the concept didn't exist in biblical times, so we don't have direct examples for it. However, there are several verses that can help us set realistic standards for dating and apply to all relationships like:

> "So flee youthful passions and pursue righteousness, faith, love, and peace, along with those who call on the Lord from a pure heart."
>
> 2 Timothy 2:22 (ESV)

> "Do not be deceived: 'Bad company ruins good morals.'"
>
> 1 Corinthians 15:33 (ESV)

"He who finds a wife finds a good thing and obtains favor from the LORD."

                                                    Proverbs 18:22 (ESV)

"Do two walk together, unless they have agreed to meet?"

                                                    Amos 3:3 (ESV)

Particularly I favor that last verse when it comes to seeking a Godly relationship because it takes two in agreement to move toward Christ together. This is the ultimate standard for a healthy relationship. Don't give up on it. Chase after God, keep moving toward Him, and pray that He'll bring someone into your life who meets you there at the feet of Jesus.

The night I knew God was hearing my prayers for a wife, I was at a wrap party for a TV show I had been working on. Completely exhausted, I was counting down the minutes until I could rest after months of being a production zombie. How could I make this party a little more bearable? Call my friends.

I felt relieved when they walked through the front door, but my breath caught when I saw in the back of the group the girl everyone had been talking about. For a moment, our eyes met across the room, confirming what no one had to tell me: *That's Rebecca.*

Section Three

HELD

Chapter 7

TRUSTING THE STORYTELLER

Cubbie

Garage Mahal. That was the name of the one-of-a-kind home makeover TV show I had been working on, transforming people's garages from cluttered-filled glorified storage units into unique works of art. From vibey man caves to state-of-the-art gyms to aerospace-themed gaming rooms, we did it all. Our biggest claim to fame was when we did an extensive build for Jay Leno at his Hollywood home.

With our run-and-gun small crew approach we were all forced to wear multiple hats on the production front, but because I had construction experience, I ended up getting roped into doing some of the build work as well. Between the twelve-to-sixteen-hour production days, and our often one-to-three a.m. (sometimes four a.m.) Foster the People rehearsals, with live performances sprinkled into the mix, I was desperate for *Garage Mahal* to finish for the season so I could catch a little break.

As a filmmaker, I tend to catalog my memories like scenes from a movie. I want to give you a glimpse of a few of the initial scenes that played out between Rebecca and me. I, of course, will be your narrator. Enjoy.

Scene 1: The Party

Pulling up to the classy mid-century modern home nestled in the Hollywood hills that hosted our *Garage Mahal* wrap party, I take in the strong silhouette of the house set against the backdrop of the sprawling city lights below. Approaching the front door, I quickly notice several of the team from the trenches of the last several months, but there's also a handful of people I don't recognize. *I guess this party was an open invite situation.* While all I really want to do is sleep, my pesky sense of loyalty got the best of me, hence my appearance at this house party. *Deep sigh.* If I was going to get through this, it would be great to have some back up. I need to bring in the troops.

Immediately, I call my roommates Kevin and Stein. "Hey, I'm at this lame party in the hills. Do you want to come?" "Sure, we love lame parties," they state before they add, "Oh, and we're hanging out with that girl from philosophy group ..." Silence as my mind swirls ... I finally reply, "Bring her along!"

Thirty minutes later, I'm standing in the drop-down living room, a key design feature of houses of that era, being talked at by a girl, a producer on the show, who has taken a liking to me. The interest is not reciprocated so I am relieved when in walk my buddies Stein (a former model who is turning the heads of everyone in the room) and Kevin, both with flowing blond locks and bronzed skin from hours on the beach volleyball court (the perfect distraction). *I'm saved!*

Trailing slightly behind Kevin is a stunning masterpiece of God's creation. As she crosses the threshold, time slows to a crawl. Over a slow exhale ... *That's her.* Her gentle gaze gracefully sweeps across the room until our eyes lock. Time stops. The thumping music fades to a muffled murmur as we share a brief moment that felt like an eternity. It was magic.

And just like that our moment is broken. The scene rapidly ramps back to twenty-four frames a second and the crack of music resumes at full volume as I notice the leader of the philosophy group on the heels of Rebecca. He's putting off a strong "I'm with this one" vibe. My heart sinks but is quickly resuscitated as I see Rebecca making her way down the stairs and across the dropped living room floor right towards me. He continues to trail her.

I take a few steps and meet her halfway. "Hi, I'm Cubbie," I say even though I'm fairly certain she already knows my name. "I'm Rebecca," she replies like she didn't know my roommates had been talking about her and trying to connect us for months. Philosophy Guy quickly tries to assert himself into the conversation. Producer Girl who has continued to hover also provides an introduction for herself. Rebecca and I say "hi," but we're not really paying attention. The world doesn't exist outside of this moment, this conversation, this woman.

Philosophy Guy and Producer Girl continue to buzz around in attempts to secure our attention, but to no avail. We are locked in. Rebecca and I have just met, yet I feel like I have known her forever. It's so natural talking to her that we stand right there in the living room and chat for at least an hour. She gently peppers me with questions and is genuinely curious about my life. Who was I? What was I up to? I'm excited to tell her about how things are picking up for the band. I ask her questions in return. I want to know everything about her, but I'm trying to not be over the top or read too much into how easy this conversation is flowing. But something inside (maybe it's the butterflies I've had since I first locked eyes with her) tells me this is amazing. Rebecca is special.

Somewhere in the middle of the conversation she asks if I have any shows coming up in the area. "Yes! We're playing the Silver Lake Lounge in a couple weeks. It's a pretty historic venue and should be fun. It's actually our last show before we head to South by Southwest in Austin." She replies enthusiastically, "Wow, I'd love to be there!" While her response was flattering, I honestly don't take a lot of stock in it. For one, I'm trying not to get my hopes up, and two, this is LA, The Land of Unfulfilled Commitments. Everybody says "I'll be there!" only to never show up. Regardless, I reply, "Awesome, I'll put you on the list!"

Philosophy Guy gave up and retreated to a sofa in the corner. Producer Girl also lost steam and slipped into the background somewhere. Before we knew it, the party died down around us. People are leaving, the music is turning off. We feel like we have stepped into a time capsule only to emerge and find the remnants of a party that once was. We make our way to the door as my mind and heart swirl. *Do I get her number? Do we just say bye and see what happens?* And in a moment of complete confidence that if this thing was right, that I didn't need to stress about it, my decision was made. As we pause before parting ways to our respective cars, with a nod and a half smile I simply say, "I'll see you soon." She smiles and I notice a slight twinkle in her eye before she turns for her car.

As I make my way to my truck, my mind returns to our conversation about the Silver Lake Lounge. *I wonder if she'll actually show up?* Maybe she was just being cordial. Or maybe she is different. As I wind my way out of the hills, I hope for the latter because I already can't wait to see her again.

Scene 2: The Show

The Foster the People show at the Silver Lake Lounge is a packed house. There's a line around the block just to get in, and the coolest hipster LA band, Deep Sea Diver, is opening for us. While they're kicking off their set, I'm sitting backstage replaying my conversation I had with Rebecca for the millionth time in my head. As it did every time I revisited that night, my stomach drops ... Once again, I'm confronted with the fact that I literally talked about myself for the majority of the conversation. For a guy who rarely has any inclination to ever talk about himself (I realize the irony of this statement as I write these words ... trust me, this is weird for me), I did a pretty good job hogging the conversation and making it all about me. Perhaps it was the nerves. Perhaps it was the excitement of the band and all the doors God seemed to be opening. Or perhaps it was because she just asked me a lot of questions. Regardless, I convinced myself for the millionth time that I'd blown my one shot with her and there's no way she'd be showing up. I'm sure she thinks I'm completely full of myself.

Deep Sea Diver wraps their set and we head out to do a changeover. My bandmates and I are pulling out our instruments and getting set up onstage. I happen to glance out into the crowd at one point, and ... there she is. She's here! I can't believe she actually showed up! My blood is pumping as we kick off the first song. Here I am, playing a classic LA venue, full of the coolest raw-denim-wearing, clever-tattoo-toting people in town but I only care about one. The beautiful woman I keep making eye contact with right in the middle of the crowd throughout the night, re-communicating the clear connection between us.

Riding the buzz that comes from playing an adrenaline-filled show in front of a room packed with rabid fans, I head offstage to see my parents who also attended the performance. I had mentioned to them there was a very small chance a girl I was interested in might be there that night. So, when Rebecca emerges from the venue and joins us on the sidewalk just outside, they are stoked. Hugs all around! My parents tell me I did a great job and can tell there's someone else I may want to spend the rest of my evening with. Besides, they had a two-hour drive back to San Diego. We say our goodbyes and I see them off.

There are pool tables in the back of the venue and Rebecca and I make our way into another easy conversation as we pick up pool sticks and start to play. Midnight has come and gone and we're starving. So, we join some friends at an extra-long table and order a mess of Thai food, which I soon learn is Rebecca's favorite. Through bites of our late-night meal, Rebecca reveals she has to be at the airport in a few hours for her next show. "I'll take you to the airport."

It's a genuine offer, but an offer that literally makes no sense. She lived in Manhattan Beach, which was probably about a seven- or eight-minute drive to Los Angeles International Airport (LAX). I lived in Hollywood, about a forty-eight-minute commute. "No, you really don't have to do that. It's a super-quick cab ride for me!" (Yes, people, this was pre-Uber.) "No, no, no," I retort with a smile. "I'd really like to give you a ride to the airport." With a smile that held the weight of multiple emotions, she finally replies, "All right, if you really want to do that." I do. I definitely want to do that. Finally, I get Rebecca's number, and we say our goodbyes.

I'm overcome with utter exhaustion. My eyelids are barely open as I set my alarm on my phone, trusting it will wake me in just a couple hours so I can get Rebecca to the airport like I promised. *What a night.*

Scene 3: The Cab Chase

Is that my alarm? I can hear it going off in my dream before I snap into a half-wakeful state. I roll over to look at my phone. Long sigh as I turn off my alarm. *Six o'clock.* Brief moment as reality comes into focus. Panic. *Wait! It's six o'clock!?* In my exhaustion I had set my alarm for when I needed to be at Rebecca's front door instead of when I needed to wake up to get there in time.

I jump out of bed and hop into my truck faster than I even knew was possible when Rebecca calls. "I'm coming but ... I'm running just a little bit late," I admit, flying down the interstate at (at least) ninety-five miles an hour (something I do not recommend). "I can still make it." Optimistically, I keep driving and checking in with her.

"I'm going to have to grab a cab," she finally responds.

"No, I'm going to make it."

It's eventually more than clear that I'm not going to make it, and she orders the cab. "I'm still coming to say goodbye," I proclaim in response to the defeat of being beat by a cab driver.

"Oh, okay, cool," Rebecca concludes. There's a tinge of doubt in her voice, and I completely get it. For a guy that prides himself in the truth of his word, I feel I have completely blown it ... again! I'm now fully determined to make it to the airport.

Finally, I get off the freeway and start heading into the airport when a cab pulls right in front of me. There's someone sitting in the back of this particular cab who has a strikingly similar silhouette to the girl I was just talking to. I call Rebecca. "Hey, I think I'm right behind you ..." "What? No way!" She turns to look out the back window of the cab and waves. *What are the odds? I can't believe that this might actually work out.*

As we pull up to the American terminal, Rebecca gets out of the cab and I park my truck in the departures unloading zone. The moment I've been waiting for all morning finally is here, severely blundered, but here nonetheless. I run to her and give her a hug. "I'm so sorry. I'm the biggest idiot in the world." There is a strange glitch in reality that morning as there are absolutely no LAX traffic enforcers barking at everyone to "keep it going." That just doesn't happen. Rebecca and I are able to enjoy a few brief but beautiful minutes together. We get her bags inside. We check her in. I hug her again just before she walks through a security check. I then watch the woman of my dreams disappear into a sea of travelers.

Rebecca

At the time our stories collided at that party, I lived in Manhattan Beach. It was a fun area to be single in—a more relaxed part of LA but still close enough to everything that you could feel the energetic hum of the city. From my apartment that I shared with two roommates, I could see the beach and the coffee shop that I often visited. I would rollerblade in the sun along the strand, a paved walkway that ran right along the ocean. It was all pretty dreamy and one of the sweetest times in my life.

One of my roommates, Lila Rose, an early twenties pro-life activist whose ministry Live Action was in the early stages of really taking off, invited me to a philosophy group. The group had been created for young creatives in LA to lay a foundation for theology through philosophy. It sounded really interesting to me, so I jumped right in. Due to her busy schedule, I don't remember my roommate attending with me much. However, I ended up becoming a regular part of "Philosophy" as we called it and became good friends with a lot of the people there, especially two guys, named Stein and Kevin.

One night we were hanging out and they said, "Our friend Cubbie is at a party in the (Hollywood) Hills and wants to see if we all want to come hang with him." I was down for it. On the way, they told me, "All right. Cubbie is one of our best friends and he's a total stud." I think they may have even gone as far as to tell me that Cubbie was "the hottest guy we know." And for character quality measures they added, "But he's also a really, really good dude." From their creative description, I was definitely intrigued.

As soon as I entered the house, I locked eyes with Cubbie across the room. It was really a magical moment and one where, though I didn't know it, I was actually living my song, "Waiting for the look in your eyes, when we meet for the first time." As we started our conversation, I was instantly attracted to him but also to Cubbie's quiet strength and self-confidence. I had sensed insecurity in a lot of the guys I had previously dated and because of that I felt I had to be smaller and quieter when I was with them. I would soon get to know that Cubbie, on the other hand, made me feel calm and at peace. He left space for my strengths and the fullness of my personhood without being intimidated. He gave me room to be fully myself.

From our hour and a half conversation, I could tell Cubbie was a deep well. He had the confidence of someone beyond his years and that was mysterious and intriguing. I wanted to know what he'd been through that had built that strength. I left the wrap party that night admitting to myself that I liked this guy. Stein and Kevin were right: he was super attractive, exactly my type. But there was so much more to this Cubbie Fink than just a handsome face. There was a solidness, depth, and wisdom about him that I found equally appealing; he was a *man* in the truest sense of the word.

And yes, as Cubbie's rendition of our first few interactions indicates, I attend his performance at the Silver Lake Lounge, connect with him afterwards, and become even more impressed with this man I had just met. I also went from questioning how much he liked me when Cubbie didn't show up to moments later witnessing him chasing my cab the next morning at LAX. What guy does that? I was impressed that he didn't give up and I felt pursued in the best way. Out of these awkwardly funny but also heartfelt moments, we started dating.

I had dated (or courted) a reasonable number of guys in my twenties and early thirties. On those dates I'd visited waterfalls, dressed up to go to nice restaurants, or traveled to interesting spots and had romantic moments in idealistic locations. However, none of these men had stolen my heart. Up until I met Cubbie, I had never fallen in love. What's ironic is that when I was finally dating the love of my life, our relationship didn't really resemble a montage from a romantic comedy movie. Rarely did we dress up and go out on the town; often we didn't even go out to eat. We sat on the couch at the apartment, talked, and watched movies. Sometimes we walked on the beach, went to a show together, or grabbed food from our favorite local All-American restaurant down the street.

Often, we just rested together. I was still burnt out after nearly twenty years of doing music, and finances were tight for Cubbie, so we mostly relaxed and became a haven for each other. There was a safety in our chill groove that worked for us both because our schedules and lives had been, and often continued to be, so intense. Outside of a few extravagant dating stories, we just lived life. For us both, it seemed like it was enough to just simply be together.

Hopeless Romantic
Cubbie

I'm definitely the hopeless romantic type. Growing up, I for the most part never dated casually. I always sensed a weight about it. That got even heavier after my Jesus encounter. To me, I felt everything about dating should be done with purpose. Women should be treated with respect, and dating should always be with the perspective that there could be at least the potential of marriage.

While it was hard for me to wrap my head around the idea of dating just for fun, I did want to have fun on dates. So, when Rebecca's birthday rolled around after we had been together a few months, I began to pull together a fun surprise.

That summer, the band rented a cabin for a long weekend retreat near Big Bear Lake just a couple of hours outside of Los Angeles. It was a short walking distance from the water, so when Rebecca called, I decided to have our conversation standing on a dock. It was a perfect summer evening with a gorgeous sunset reflecting off the still water. In front of me was another dock with two people sitting cross-legged at the end completely absorbed in each other's gaze. All I could think about was wanting to gift this moment to Rebecca, to be sitting with her on the dock, looking into each other's eyes and talking. So, mid-conversation I switched over to the camera on my phone and snapped a quick picture of the couple.

Rebecca and I both loved spending time together by the water and this photo would represent a piece of our relationship. A gift! To give her this moment for her birthday, I devised a technique where I pulled the picture to

Photoshop, enhanced the black, blue, and gold tones, and amped up the saturation to give it a vintage flair. Once the coloring had transformed the couple into a silhouette backdropped by a vibrant lake, I digitally cut the image into sixteen different squares. Then, I took the files to Kinko's and had each individual square printed out. Using Mod Podge, a type of glue you can use to decoupage anything, I pasted them all onto a giant forty-inch by forty-inch canvas.

I also knew Rebecca loved German apple pancakes. So, when July 26 (her actual birthday) rolled around, I showed up at her front door at eight o'clock in the morning with a freshly purchased cast-iron skillet to make her a puffy, oven-baked pancake, and a bouquet of flowers wrapped and tucked behind my back.

I found "The Best German Apple Pancake Recipe" on the internet and it did turn out to be delicious. After cooking together and enjoying a sweet morning moment, I moved on to present number two, the big canvas. I told her all about taking the photo during our phone conversation in Big Bear and how I made it with the intention of saving the moment. She loved it! Just when she assumed there couldn't possibly be anything else, I came out with, "All right, I've got a day trip planned for us!"

Somewhere along the line I picked up that Rebecca had a dream of someday going hang gliding. With the learning curve on a hang glider being pretty steep, I found the next best thing, paragliding. I knew of a place just north of downtown San Diego. We'd be strapped to an instructor as we used the updraft coming off the towering ocean cliffs to fly up and down the coastline.

I knew Rebecca was adventurous, so I didn't tell her exactly what we were about to do as we drove south towards Black's Beach. As we neared the bluff, and she could see paragliders peppering the horizon line, it clicked. "Oh my goodness. Are we doing this?" she asks, eyes glistening with a bit of nervous excitement. "Yeah," I confirm. "We're doing this."

We got strapped in to separate pilots, they threw out the chutes, and we ran and jumped off the cliff. We glided high above the surfers and beach goers below, catching updrafts when we would start to sink and climbed back into the air. We had a blast. Rebecca has always been an incredible mix of cautious and daring to me.

For our final stop on her grand birthday adventure, we went to my parents' house. She had met them before briefly at the show in Silver Lake, but this was my first time bringing her home. At my parents' house (because I didn't have a real kitchen in my tiny, hotel-sized apartment), I wanted to give her a taste of her homeland, Australian sausage rolls. While she may have been the better chef whipping up some of her native cuisine, part of her gift was me cooking for her. So, she kept me company as I set to work tying a bow on the end of a multi-layered birthday surprise with a homemade dinner.

Rebecca

I was utterly amazed at the layers of joy and wonder that Cubbie created for me on my birthday. He was so caring and thoughtful and already knew all these things that I enjoyed and was bringing them to life! He had crafted all these incredible experiences for me. I was also impressed by how confidently he was pursuing me. With any other guy, these extravagant gestures so early in our relationship might have freaked me out. But with Cubbie, they didn't. There was something so special and different for me with him. I had been praying about our relationship, asking God to help me lower the wall of fear I had built up around my heart ... enough to truly fall in love.

While I struggled with feeling like I was not enough in some areas of my life, I also thought I was "too much" emotionally for guys. I've always been quite sensitive and can be reasonably intense. In past relationships, this had either intimidated guys or I felt like I needed to try to hide my heart. God was slowly answering that prayer as I began to care more for Cubbie—one date and day at a time.

Taking the risk to be vulnerable with my heart wasn't always easy. As I started to let my guard down and allow my mind to venture into thoughts like *He could be the one*, I had quite a few moments where I became fearful and emotional. (We promised you guys we'd be raw and honest, so here are the waterworks that happened on that birthday date, amidst all the sunshine and butterflies.)

On our drive from LA to San Diego on my birthday, I started crying in the car. I had an expectation that if you're meant to be together forever, you talked all the time. Mainly because that's what we did on car trips growing up with my family. We kids would fight for a spot on the middle bench seat between my parents and we chatted the whole time. However, during most of the drive that day, Cubbie was almost silent. I thought something was off between us and I became upset. I had let this guy into my heart and now something was going wrong. If we couldn't talk freely, and my attempts to connect weren't being warmly responded to, maybe "we" were not going to work!

I turned my head toward the window as silent tears started to trickle down my face, hoping to hide my emotions from him. But when I couldn't help my sniffling, he noticed my tears and pulled over. He calmed me down and reassured me that he just doesn't talk a ton; he wasn't upset. With his family and when he's with the people he cares about, silence is a good thing. To him, being able to just be in each other's presence, and that be enough, means you get one another. I hadn't thought of it like that before. That drive was the moment Cubbie and I really began to learn from one another about the give and take of a healthy relationship.

Cubbie let me be me, and I was going to let him be him (even if that meant some quiet car rides).

The Talk

My family liked to go all out when we turned twenty-one, so we planned a family trip to stay on a houseboat on Lake Powell for my little brother Josh's twenty-first birthday. Every prior family holiday I had shown up alone. It's not that I wasn't dating, it's just that I never was ready to bring any of the guys I had been seeing to vacation with my family. But this time was different. I was finally excited to bring my boyfriend to a family trip! So I invited Cubbie to join us for a week of family fun on the lake.

After moving band rehearsals around, Cubbie agreed to come and meet us on Lake Powell. The views were stunning, and we were all having a great time, except that Cubbie kept venturing off with my brothers to go water skiing and speed boating. Sure, I invited him to do some family bonding, but I didn't feel that I was being prioritized in the way I had hoped to be.

We were supposed to connect here. This was going to be so romantic. *Is he not as into me as I am into him? Am I at risk of being rejected?* These concerns were based on insecurity, I knew it. So much of our dating up until this point had been incredible. Cubbie was an amazing man, I never doubted that. However, I was at a fragile time in my life. This "glass half full," optimistic girl who may have otherwise brushed this off was struggling with insecurities and self-doubt. I didn't want to be a needy girlfriend, but I had to talk to him about this. I thought I might be falling in love, and I wasn't going to let missed expectations take us out. I hoped we would be able to discuss how I was feeling when we could grab a few moments away from my family, but we weren't able to make peace with anything before we left.

After the trip, Cubbie remained in LA with Foster the People and I was away to work on recording an album in Nashville, feeling vulnerable in my singing and also in our relationship. Our communication was suffering because, similarly to our differences in expectations in the car, we couldn't chat well on the phone. (I came to find out later that he just really struggled to connect over the phone, disliked it strongly, and would have much preferred to be in person.) Every time we talked long distance, his tone hurt me. I could feel my heart retreating and I started to think we weren't moving at the same speed down this relationship track. I had to put the brakes on and protect my heart ... and I was instinctively pulling back already.

I expressed to Cubbie that I was struggling and hurt. I needed to take a break from communicating for a little bit. He tried to reach out, but I was unresponsive for a few days, which was highly unusual for me. It wasn't that I was trying to manipulate him. Between the questions that the Lake Powell trip had brought up, and the hard phone chats, my heart just needed to hit pause. We did make a plan, though, to meet up when I got back. I wasn't done. We just needed to talk in person.

Cubbie

We decided to meet at an Italian restaurant in downtown San Diego and took a table outside. Rebecca sweetly but boldly told me, "I've been thinking and praying about us and I have some things I need to share." The hustle and bustle of the main street beside us dissipated into the background. I hung on the weight of her every word because I could tell they conveyed the heaviness of her heart. I had felt the weight of her distance. This was serious.

"Look. I know I will be okay, that God will take care of me even if this doesn't work out," Rebecca said. "But I would like for it to work out." Her words lingered for a moment as I gathered the thoughts and words I too had prepared.

The few days that preceded this talk, I did some deep soul searching. Through my prayerful introspection, I recognized I had some serious fears about jumping all in. Rebecca needed all of me and part of "my all" was still tied up with my ex-girlfriend from South Africa. I had fond memories of her and was grateful for our relationship and the standard she created in my heart. That example wisely kept me from settling for less than God's best several times along my way to Rebecca. But what I truly came to understand was it was time to release her, and in turn free up the piece of my heart that the imprint of that relationship was still occupying. Rebecca not only met the bar, she surpassed it. It was this that I shared with Rebecca that night. God gave me the strength to let go and to jump all in. I gave Rebecca my heart.

We both took the risk to have the difficult conversation, but it was worth it because "The Talk" became a definitive moment for our relationship. We started properly texting and talking because I knew communication was important to her. In several messages, I even became expressive and started using smiley faces and exclamation marks. It was freeing and fun!!!

But seriously, we had learned to speak each other's language and it was then that our conversation and connection really took off. I continued to learn her heart and the full breadth of emotions she experienced. She sought to more deeply understand my introverted tendencies and started to give me time to decompress and process. Rebecca embodied everything I had ever hoped and prayed for. We had our ups and downs. I had no expectations for our romance to be a fairy tale. All I knew was that as life threw us the good and the bad, I wanted to walk through it with her.

The rest is history.

I was the bass, holding us down, giving us a steady foundation. Rebecca was the melody, the heartbeat, helping us find our way through.

Chapter 8

WAIT NO MORE

Cubbie

Nine months into dating Rebecca I knew, beyond a shadow of a doubt, that I wanted to marry her. But asking David Smallbone if I could marry his oldest daughter needed to happen in person. Rebecca had invited me to join her and her family for Christmas at the family farm in Nashville. Perfect, I would make the ask then and there.

I had been considering a handful of proposal ideas, which I eventually narrowed down to two. One was at the 1920s theater that was in the process of being restored in quaint downtown Franklin, Tennessee. I could rent it out and we could watch *It's a Wonderful Life*. I was thinking through how, where, and when I would get down on one knee when the plan fell through. On to the next one ...

I could build a scene in the woods … a candlelit path that would lead to a bonfire and a Christmas tree with candles all around it. Under the tree would be a series of gifts. The final gift, of course, would be the ring. Okay, this one was doable. So I started to set my plan into motion.

While we were staying at the farm, I snuck off when I could to scout out the perfect spot, but I couldn't let anyone know what I was up to. Rebecca's parents had no idea I was thinking about marriage. Heck, Rebecca and I hadn't even said "I love you" to each other yet, let alone had the marriage talk. Minor details.

On one of my adventures in the woods, I found *the* spot: a little clearing with the perfect amount of space for my tree and candle setup. I ran to the store to grab a bunch of candles and gathered some rocks for a fire ring. I found the perfect little living Christmas tree and decorated it with all the bells and whistles. For three days, my secret went undiscovered while I obsessively checked the forecast that to my dismay had been calling for rain.

While I patiently asked God to clear the skies, I used my time to plan the ask with Rebecca's dad. It was getting down to the wire and I needed his blessing. He walked the dogs every evening, so I decided on the night before Christmas Eve I would join him.

He totally knew something was up the moment I asked if I could go, but he agreed to let me venture out with him and the dogs anyway. As David started to put on his jacket and grab the leashes, I bundled up too and we headed out the door. Rebecca's brother Daniel was in the kitchen and said, "Oh, are you guys going to walk the dogs? I'll come with you." To which David replied, "I think Cubbie wants to talk to me about something." He totally knew.

We began strolling along and engaging in casual conversation. At a break in shooting the breeze, I realized that was my moment. "Well, I'd actually like to chat with you about something." My heart was beating a million miles an hour as I launched into my lengthy, rehearsed speech asking him for his blessing to marry his daughter. He said nothing for at least ten to fifteen paces. Finally, he stopped and pulled his hood back, "What was that?" he asked. There was no way I could repeat the full speech! "Do you mean, like the last part, or the whole thing?" "Just the last part," he replied. "Can I marry your daughter?" His reply, "That's what I thought you said." He pulled his hood back up against the cold and kept walking.

But as we circled the entire forty acres back to the house, David dropped on me all his wisdom about marriage. He shared with me Rebecca's passion for children and how she was going to want kids right away. She was going to need someone to support that dream. He wrapped up with a long pause and then "I'm going to have to think about it. I'm going to need to talk to Helen." "Okay, fair enough." I genuinely appreciated the advice and that was the best reply I could think of in the tension of the moment. I went to bed that night feeling optimistic but equally nervous. If David had major concerns, he would have raised them in our conversation, which bolstered my optimism a bit. But my nerves were charged with the fact that he gave me no firm answer. This was in no way a done deal.

The next day, I didn't see David until mid-morning. He must have been running errands or doing something around the farm until then. The stress was really beginning to mount as my window for my proposal plan was closing quick. When we finally bumped into each other, he said, "Talked to Helen." He then offered me a head nod, a nonverbal "We're good." I was flooded with relief and excitement. The plan was on!

Operation Proposal

Operation Proposal was in full effect. So I went back to base camp, my little clearing up the hill and in the woods, to make the final arrangements. As I gazed up at the thick, dark clouds, I continued my prayers for the rain to hold off. Pulling out my weather app, I saw something no short of a miracle … the rain was supposed to turn into snow.

Rebecca

The first snow of the season started flurrying down just before Christmas Eve service. The entire family emerged from the church to a beautiful blanket of snow. We felt like we were in a Hallmark movie. It rarely snows in Franklin, let alone on Christmas Eve. Little did I know, God was setting the stage for Cubbie's proposal.

After dinner, we all piled into the living room to watch *It's a Wonderful Life*. It was a cozy holiday evening and Cubbie even dozed off a bit during the movie. I'm still amazed that Cub was able to fall asleep right before he proposed to me. He didn't even know for sure that I would say "yes"! Prior to this point, we had not said "I love you" to each other. We would say "I like you a lot a lot," which for us was the same thing. Again, this speaks to the security of my man ... *and* his ability to fall asleep anywhere. Needless to say, I wasn't expecting a wild turn of events to take place when Cubbie asked me after the movie to go on a walk. "That'd be so nice in the snow," I commented.

It was after midnight and the full moon was casting sparkling light on the freshly fallen snow, making everything look soft and enchanted. It was a winter wonderland. As soon as I agreed to the walk, Cubbie told me he'd be right back and set off like a shot into the woods. *What was he up to?* Half an hour passed and he finally returned. "Ready to go?" he asked. "I want to show you something." "Yes. Let's go," I said as he handed me a thermos full of steaming tea and we headed out.

As we were strolling hand-in-hand, I could tell Cubbie was guiding me toward the open fields on my parents' farm. When we crested a hill, I saw it. There were at least one hundred candles lighting a pathway near the woods, surrounding a lit fire pit, and ending at a charming little Christmas tree with presents underneath.

"Merry Christmas," Cubbie said softly as I looked around in amazement. He sat me down on a log by the fire and said, "I got a few gifts for you," as if setting up this Christmas-card-cover-worthy scene wasn't enough! He had been so elaborate on my birthday I assumed he was also just going all out for Christmas. I embraced the extravagance as I opened my first gift, a beanie and mittens, because "it might be a little chilly tonight." I put them on and enjoyed the moment of us just being there by the fire sipping tea.

After a bit he said, "All right, I got another present for you." I unrolled a scroll to find a letter that Cubbie had written, sharing everything he appreciated and enjoyed most about me. He signed it *"Love,* Cubbie." This was huge. *Love.* This was the first time he had used the "L" word. "Wow, that was really beautiful. Thank you." I was just particularly amazed that my quiet boyfriend was being so expressive in his feelings for me. My heart was full!

The next present I opened was a ceramic frog. Cubbie had noticed a little statue of a frog sitting on a bench with the word "Waiting" written under it in my apartment. So, for this extremely special occasion, he bought a similar frog. Around its neck was a handwritten note that said, "Wait no more."

Reality started to sink in. *"Wait no more" ... He was not ... there's no way ...* And then Cubbie got down on one knee and pulled out a ring. "Will you marry me?" The question I'd been waiting to hear for so long, I didn't have to wait to be asked any longer. In this sacred moment, with decades of anticipation behind it, I said "yes" with a wonder-filled and joyous heart. In the earliest hours of that beautiful Christmas morning, a new and glorious day had dawned for me.

The Great Storyteller of Our Lives

The way Cubbie set up our engagement was a dream come true. It was movie-script worthy. And we headed into our engagement season hopeful for the future. However, with all that excitement, I also noticed that I was a little bit afraid.

What no one really tells you is that it's okay to have some fears pop up during your dating or engagement season, even with the "right person," because the saying that "opposites attract" is generally true. Cubbie and I were very much that.

While we've had two very different lives, I feel like he and I share the same soul. We can trust each other's intentions because our beliefs and values are so similar. But there's a lot of balance that goes into our "oneness," and we, like every other engaged couple, had to navigate our differences as we approached our wedding day.

My problems didn't magically stop the moment Cubbie slipped that beautiful engagement ring onto my finger. This was the event of my life that I was planning, and yet there was so much stress circulating at that time. My voice was still in really rough shape and I had shows. We were now having to plan a wedding and squeeze in premarital counseling in our already slammed schedules. Because of Foster the People's upcoming tour, there was only a two-week window where we could actually get married or we were going to have to wait another six months to a year.

I found myself waking up in the morning with a racing heart, the weight of this massive commitment I was about to make sitting heavy on my shoulders. Our dating journey had been a short nine months, and we still had a few areas in our relationship that could do with some pruning and growth. I'd think things like, *I love this man so much. I want to marry him.* Then I'd ask:

> *But is it right?*
> *How do you really know someone?*
> *Can you be certain they're not going to bail on you?*
> *How do you really know that your future spouse is as committed*
>   *to this covenant as you are?*
> *How do you really know who they're going to be on the other side*
>   *of marriage?*

I had to address my fears about our engagement with God because our relationship had moved forward quickly and we had spent a good part of our dating long distance. Ultimately, we were running our love off the way that we trusted each other and the soulmate connection that God had given us.

I have always believed in seeking wise counsel, so I called my longtime pastor back in Tennessee and laid out some of the fears that I was dealing with. He simply asked, "If you could marry Cubbie tomorrow, would you do it?" My instinctive answer was "Yes!" So, I was able to identify that my fear wasn't rooted in doubting Cubbie, it was spilling out of how overwhelming my life situations were. Needing more, I asked God to biblically confirm this marriage for me and He did. I received scriptures from God that brought peace. I sensed a strong Holy Spirit "yes" as I sought God about it, but I still had to choose faith over fear as we moved forward.

I tell you all this because I think it's okay to be a little bit afraid, to not have rose-colored glasses about your relationship. Be aware of its flaws and seek counsel about how to get the confirmation you need before you enter this huge commitment. Most importantly, boldly talk to God because marriage is intended to be a lasting covenant between you, your spouse, and God. There is a great weight and holy heaviness that we should feel as we move forward because it's not just a human contract like society makes it out to be. A Christian marriage is a lifelong promise to love our spouse, even in the areas we're least lovable. That's hard! Sometimes our fear points to the sincerity with which we're taking this step and our understanding that we're about to vow to make our life story about more than just ourselves.

But God is the great storyteller of our lives. The Bible, His Holy Word, is God's love story for His people. It displays His constant pursuit of us and the ultimate home He has planned for us in heaven. Whether we've known it or not, we've always been a part of the love story He's been writing throughout time. Stepping back to view engagement and marriage as a love story that's playing a part of God's greater story to save and redeem His people can feel both beautiful and a bit wild. Scary even.

Let me speak peace over you if you're experiencing fear in engagement. If you've chosen a partner who is a believer, and your relationship has been confirmed over time and through wise counsel, it's okay to move forward a little bit scared, fully aware of those spaces where you notice your differences and struggle to get along at times. We can trust God will write a beautiful story through our marriage if we give Him both our weaknesses and strengths. "For better or worse," right? After all, trusting God in our marriage through all circumstances is what we're truly committing to when we say, "I do."

Wedding Day

On April 23, 2011, we were married in San Diego, California, at the iconic Junípero Serra Museum, one of California's oldest missions that overlooks stunning views of the Mission Bay area. The building's traditional Spanish architecture with its whitewashed mud walls, small chapel, terra cotta tile roof, and long stretching courtyard made it a picturesque location for our wedding. We packed out the small mission chapel on that perfect spring afternoon with 175 people and overflowed the clay tiled patio with tables, chairs, towers of food and flowers for a reception.

Cubbie's former student pastor from his church in San Diego, Chris Schmaltz, and my pastor, Rick White, from our church, The People's Church in Franklin, Tennessee, were standing at the end of the aisle along with Cubbie and his groomsmen, all in black suits and ties. My bridesmaids in single-strap, purple-brown floor-length gowns, and the flower girl in white tulle with a flower crown, all glided into their positions. The colors in the room were balanced by white lily bridesmaids' bouquets and accents of gold. Our wedding reflected us, a blend of old souls, ancient teachings, and new life all coming together as one.

The music shifted as my dad escorted me down the aisle. I was in a classic white, strapless wedding dress with my hair curled and styled under a short veil. I felt triumphant, sentimental, and giddy with joy as I made my way down

Capturing a "happy snap" on our first official date after the airport ride debacle. Los Angeles, CA.

Celebrating my Jewish heritage and lighting the menorah with Mama. Denver, CO, age 2.

Young passions die hard ... guitars and motorcycles!

The joy of age 7 and a piggyback!

Gigging with Dad and working those rototoms. Denver, CO, age 4.

Taking a quick break from my "Bomb in the USA" bike to climb the "Winnie Cooper" tree. Bakersfield, CA, age 5.

My "human highlighter" outfit. Absolute favorite, then and now. What's not seen here are my DayGlo green shorts and Reebok tennis pumps. Epic. Disneyland Hotel, age 8.

Creative bike riding!
With my brother Joel,
ages 8 and 1.

Here I am, elementary age, pictured in my school uniform at Pacific Hills Christian School in Sydney. Such formative years, laying a foundation for a life of music and ministry!

I gave my life to Jesus at Girls Brigade meeting. Here I am in my uniform at age 9.

A San Diego Fink family Christmas photo. Got a little chilly, like 68 degrees, so Dad slipped on his jacket. Age 9.

This is our family the year after the "miraculous" Christmas of '91 featured in *Unsung Hero*. Lots of joy for these freshly arrived Australians living in the US.

Straight '90s grunge! Featured here (beyond my long hair) are my first guitar, the Memphis, and my miniature Marshall stack. Warner Springs, CA, age 12.

A game that had my heart and dedication for many years. A game that I love and deeply miss. Encinitas, CA, age 14.

A snowman for everyone!

I truly did always want us to be the kids from *The Sound of Music!* As you can see, some siblings were less than impressed with my ideas! :)

In my happy place. A nearly daily experience growing up in San Diego.

First day in South Africa. Riding up the N1 toward Paarl in the back of a truck. Cape Town, South Africa, age 19.

My trip to Calcutta, India, with Compassion to meet my sponsored child was a life-changing one!

"We're married!" The victorious moment of redemption and joy!

Another "happy snap," this time on our honeymoon. Mo'orea, French Polynesia.

Receiving our Canadian double platinum record plaque. Toronto, Canada.

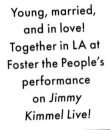

Young, married, and in love! Together in LA at Foster the People's performance on *Jimmy Kimmel Live!*

The joy of
becoming
a father.

Performing together
on the road with
FK&C Christmas 2017,
and announcing
baby Fink no. 2. Our
"spring" had begun.

Our family grows ...
with weeks-old Imogen
at her baby shower,
with big sister Gemma!

Thankful for the partnership of many decades with Focus on the Family! Our family was honored to be part of their magazine again in the spring of 2024.

the aisle to my gorgeous groom who was expressing a huge, misty-eyed grin. As I stood before my almost-husband in a moment we had both long waited and prayed for, the beginning of our wedding felt like a miracle. It was as if the whole room held their breath, eyes fixed on us, as they watched the union of a couple who kept stepping toward God and finally collided with each other.

The ceremony was full of symbolism. There were traditional teachings shared by both pastors. Cubbie and I washed each other's feet to display how we would choose to serve one another in our marriage. In place of a unity candle, we took turns pouring sand from both Australia and San Diego into a vase, revealing how our lives intertwined to become a new work of art for the glory of God. We exchanged purity rings to commemorate the ending of a long journey and the beginning of a new and more beautiful one.

Along with traditional vows, we shared our own:

"My sweet Bec, this day marks the beginning of a new chapter for us, and in the company of God, and our family, and our loved ones, these things I promise to you—to honestly seek the Lord for His guidance on how I can best care for you and lead you. To use my words to love you and encourage you. To use my touch to cherish you and adore you. To faithfully stand with you and protect you. To remind you that you are more than enough just the way you are. To be gentle and loving in the way I speak and respond to you. I promise to honor you and support you. To laugh with you and to cry with you. To hold you when you need to be held. To always find time devoted to you even amidst our crazy lives. Bec, I give you my hand, my heart, and the best of who I am from this day forward."

"This is my solemn vow to you, my beloved man, my sweet friend, my brother in Jesus, a leader whom I greatly respect, my love. I commit to cherish you above any other. To serve you with my hands, to care for you

with my body, to honor you with my words, to encourage you in your love for Jesus, to be your faithful help-mate, co-adventurer, dearest friend. I commit to be led by God's love and the guidance of the Holy Spirit as I love you.

Come what may, I am yours. My love and my heart are yours, and we are, from this day forward, one. To be your wife is my delight and the greatest joy and calling of my life. May we honor and glorify our Lord Jesus together more than we have apart. Where you go I will go and where you stay I will stay. Your people will be my people and your God will be my God."

This holy ceremony culminated in an exchange of our wedding bands. The wait was over. Cubbie could kiss me now as his wife, his bride!

Cheers erupted from the room as the pastor declared, "May we now introduce to you, Mr. and Mrs. Cubbie Fink!"

As a newly married couple, we were making our way down the aisle when Cubbie unexpectedly bent over to scoop me up in his arms. My natural reaction was to throw my fist into the air in victory. This wasn't just a celebration to close out the ceremony, it was a triumphal entry into a future we, now Mr. and Mrs. Fink, had fought for.

HELD, NOT HELD BACK

Cubbie

Before I went paragliding with Rebecca, I had been skydiving a couple times. My first experience was unique in that it was solo as opposed to a tandem jump. As a young thrill seeker, I had aspirations of getting my skydiving license, that would lead to base jumping and eventual wingsuit flying. But before all that came the first step in the accreditation process ... a solo static line jump.

When you go skydiving for the first time, you arrive as ready as you can be to fall several thousand feet from a small aircraft back to solid ground. The good news is, they don't just throw you in the air and push you out of the plane. In my case, we went through a roughly seven-hour training class that walked us through as much as you could possibly learn to prepare for a first jump. The majority of the class was spent becoming well acquainted with the mechanics, function, and operation of the parachute. By the end, I found myself stepping into the leg straps of my own parachute, hoisting it onto my back, and tightly lashing down every strap and harness to the point that I felt one with my pack. Then, I walked out on an active runway and glanced up to see small specks in the sky above ... humans falling towards the earth at around one hundred and twenty miles per hour. My heart raced in excitement as I climbed into the small aircraft and lined up with my classmates. Just like that, we were airborne and climbing to altitude.

I was the last to board, which meant I would be the first one out. I was sitting on the floor of the plane facing the tail, with my left hip against the jump door. I can guarantee you that as the instructor pushed that door open, and I got my first glance of the landscape below and just how far I was about to fall, the last thing I was thinking was, *Man, I wish I had fewer restraints. Can I loosen these harnesses? You know what, this parachute is just a little too uncomfortable. I'll just jump without it.* No. If anything, I was double checking that all my harnesses were as secure and tight as they could be. My life depended on it.

But so many of us are doing this when it comes to relationships. We've opened the door to the dating world and want to ask God to loosen up. Are all these boundaries necessary? Can we just jump into dating and marriage without You? Might be more fun!

Like the parachute, God wants to stay locked in with us throughout our lives, not to restrain us, but to protect us. He is our ultimate lifesaving protection. He knows what we need to reach our wedding day, and ultimately our great reception into heaven, safely.

I know. "Safe" can sound so boring, but when you hit the ground in one piece after falling through the sky, you celebrate. Everything that kept you locked in releases you into that moment when you get to joyously reflect with all your friends and family that you just jumped out of a plane and lived to tell the tale.

This is how it felt at Rebecca and my reception. We had locked in with God when we opened the door to dating. As we surveyed the jump we were about to make, we knew we couldn't do it without Him. So, we didn't. We let Him hold us. We saw His boundaries, and to the best of our abilities, we clung to them. The life of our relationship depended on it.

My determination to do things right in our relationship stemmed from knowing what it was like to have jumped without Jesus. There were times where God didn't give me the thumbs-up yet and I toppled out anyway. Like Adam and Eve, I have heard Satan whisper in my ear, "Did God really say, you must not ...?" And I wondered if being held by God and His Word was holding me back (Gen. 3:1).

If you've ever jumped without Jesus, you know that at first it might seem fun. We can feel cool in the independence of what we're doing or navigating on our own. But, I always made impact with a problem that I, in my own strength, couldn't handle. I either got myself or someone hurt. In the end, I wish in those occasions that I would have done it God's way. I think after biting the forbidden fruit and witnessing the consequences, Adam and Eve probably said the same thing.

When we hear, "Did God really say, you must not ...?" we have to remember that God is never giving us boundaries to constrain us but to protect us.

We have to talk back to the sneaky serpent crafting cultural lies that make us question God's ways and say, "Yes, God did really say that. And it's for a good reason."

Rebecca and I fought hard against some of the dating norms that went against God's Word while we dated. In LA, no one would have blinked an eye if we would have moved in together. We easily could have really done whatever we wanted. But we trusted God and His Word. As a result, we felt freedom as we fell in love. Sure, we had struggles, but we knew our hearts were cared for. We were safe. So, when we finally landed on our wedding day, we celebrated in a big way. God had seen us through every moment, and we were able to walk into our future together with fists in the air. We jumped into dating the Jesus Way and now live to tell of how that has blessed our marriage in more ways than we can count.

Rebecca

As we headed into our reception, we got to celebrate not only our marriage, but every moment God had orchestrated in our lives. He held us in purity until He brought us together.

When we think of God holding us in purity, our culture would say God is holding us back. But we don't feel that way. Not having sex until marriage is simply a delay of gratification, a trade for something better, our sinful nature given up for His true, good, and beautiful way. The same goes for any sin really. God asks us to abstain from all kinds of things like "sexual immorality, impurity and debauchery; idolatry and witchcraft; hatred, discord, jealousy, fits of rage, selfish ambition, dissensions, factions and envy; drunkenness, orgies, and the like" because he's got something better planned (Gal. 5:19–21). God doesn't tell us "don't do that" to be mean or keep something from us. He asks us to avoid sin because He's protecting us.

My parents had a unique approach to talking to my siblings and I about this topic. They'd say, "You could go out and party. You can drink and do drugs and have sex outside of marriage. You could do any of that, but like God and Scripture, we would advise you not to. These things will possibly lead to some form of addiction, some form of getting yourself in trouble, you'll probably make decisions that you don't want to make. You could possibly find yourself pregnant outside of marriage or have to face harsh emotional or mental consequences. We will let you choose because God lets you choose. But we want you to know the potential outcome." We are free to choose the trajectory of our lives. The reality of what we're actually deciding between is to be held by God or by the consequences of our sin.

At our wedding, though we hadn't done everything perfectly, we celebrated many years of deciding to honor God, our future spouse, and our own bodies. The foundation of love is trust. We were able to trust each other deeply early on in our marriage because we'd been practicing faithfulness and integrity for the many years before we met. As we held each other, we knew God didn't hold us back all those years, He set us free to enjoy this moment and our marriage.

Being held by God is a concept that reaches far beyond just our relationships into our everyday lives. The world can be a scary, dark place. There's a lot to navigate. When we're committed to honoring God (like Cubbie shared in his skydiving analogy) there's a protection.

For Cubbie and I both, God guarded our hearts and bodies by allowing us to grasp the concept of the sanctity of marriage and knowing that sex was reserved for our future spouse early on in our teenage years. We both faced temptation to drop our physical boundaries, as friends started exploring sex in high school and it became normalized in relationships in adulthood. But we always had a determination to do things God's way and great friends who made us feel like we weren't crazy because they shared that same commitment to purity. Where culture saw sex as casual, we had a core group of people around us that upheld it as holy.

No one is perfect. We've all fallen into the trap of sin in our lives and have had to face the consequences of our decisions. When I'm tempted to think that God is holding me back and I want to take what I think I need instead of trusting God's way, I think about the conversations I'll have to have with my children one day.

Even before I was married, I thought about my future kids and how someday I would want to talk to them about the way I chose to live. I've always wanted to be able to tell them that God held me in the palm of His hand, He protected me and guided me as I honored Him, and I got to walk into marriage with their father in freedom and trust. I wanted to be able to challenge them to seek God and discover how His best for their lives is better than anything they could ever try to create for themselves. It may mean waiting, but the wait is worth it.

God promises us that He is working all things out for His glory and our good (Rom. 8:28). This is sometimes hard to believe when you're watching your friends enjoy things that the Bible warns against or calls sin. Trust me, I get that. In those moments, may we remember God isn't keeping us from enjoyment, He's protecting us so we can experience all life has to offer in freedom. I love how Psalm 63:8 says, "My soul clings to you; your right hand upholds me" (ESV). God is holding us up. He's not holding us back, He's setting us free.

Section Four

KNOWN

Chapter 9

THE BLISSFUL YEARS

Cubbie

The first few years of our marriage were an absolute whirlwind of once-in-a-lifetime experiences and milestone moments. Years prior, on a pit stop making my way back to South Africa, I was able to visit the Eiffel Tower in Paris for the first time. I was alone, and as I reached the highest platform of the tower, I remember having the very distinct thought: *This is pretty awesome, but it would be even better if I were able to share this moment with someone.* The fact that I was now able to experience so many of those surreal moments in that time with Rebecca was such a gift. While I will always view that season with affection and deep gratitude, I honestly don't tell too many stories or talk about this pretty epic time in my life all that often. For one, so much of what we were able to do feels a bit out of touch with everyday reality. Secondly, I am definitely overcautious about what could be perceived as "name dropping." Yet, with the hope of giving you a behind-the-scenes glimpse of my life, and share some of the surreal joy of that time, I thought it would be fun to revisit a handful of standout memories.

One of the first "big moments" along the way, which happened shortly before Rebecca and I got married (six days to be exact), was playing the Coachella music festival in Indio, California. Growing up in Southern California, Coachella was always "The" festival to go to, and the thought of ever playing there felt completely unattainable. After signing with Columbia Records, we embarked on our first full US tour. Nothing glamorous. A clunky fifteen-seater van, a U-Haul trailer, cheap hotels, and a bunch of small and smelly bars and venues, but we loved every second of it. After our final show of that tour, we flew directly from the East Coast to Indio and were seemingly thrown straight onto stage at ... Coachella! We went from play-ing to a room of about one hundred people the night before (status quo for the shows of that tour), to a festival tent packed with roughly ten thousand screaming festival goers. It seemed that all the buzz and momentum from online, magazines, and radio-play culminated in that moment and created a wave that carried us for the following several years.

Other memorable high points included getting to record a live session at Abbey Road Studios (yes, THE Abbey Road Studios where the Beatles recorded 190 of their 210 songs), playing a festival at the base of Mount Fuji in Japan, Lollapalooza in São Paulo (where we played to a crowd of nearly a hundred thousand people), riding motorcycles and surfing our brains out in Bali, Indonesia, swimming in the Marina Bay Sands infinity pool in Singapore (if you haven't seen it, look it up, it's insane!), exploring several bucket list cities around the world, playing nearly every late night television show, including *Saturday Night Live*, and a little "second honeymoon" for Rebecca and I in Fiji. One of my fondest memories of that season was playing to a sold-out crowd at the legendary Red Rocks amphitheater in Colorado. The crowd included my entire family sitting in the first few rows, in a venue that I can only imagine resembles the throne room of the Creator. I was on the brink of tears the entire show.

Another fun story was when we were invited to play at Elton John's charity event in LA, which was a huge honor. Halfway through sound check, I turned around to see the legend himself, Elton John, sitting on my bass amp happily bobbing his head along to our music. It became even more mind-blowing when guests started showing up for the party and in walked my childhood crush Danica McKellar, the actress who played Winnie Cooper in one of my favorite TV shows, *The Wonder Years*. At that point with the band, I had met, conversed with, worked with, and gotten to know a lot of well-known people. I had never really been thrown off in the process, but if I am completely honest, when I saw Winnie (I mean Danica) walk in, I got so nervous I thought I was going to pee my pants.

Rebecca was with me and could see I was clearly freaking out. "What's going on?" she asked. With a look of shock I replied, "Winnie Cooper is here!" Rebecca just casually stated, "Oh yeah. You've got to meet her." She proceeded to drag me by the arm across the room to Danica and, as if they were old friends, said, "Hey, Danica, this is my husband, Cubbie." I, however, was not as cool as I would have hoped and ended up spilling my guts about how I attempted to re-create an iconic scene from an episode of *The Wonder Years* to win my first kiss.

"So, you remember when you and Kevin kissed for the first time?" I asked her, heart racing and a bit short of breath. "Yes," she said with an amused half smile on her face. "I had it all ... a bench under a cool tree, the closest thing I could find to a letterman jacket, a beautiful sunset. All the elements I thought you needed for your first kiss to just, you know, happen. But shortly after stepping into the perfectly orchestrated scene with a neighbor girl that I liked, she quickly got bored, obviously not noticing the time and effort that went into that moment, and said, 'Let's go ride bikes.'" Danica laughed and responded, "Oh that's really cute," either because she actually thought it was funny or she was just trying to be nice. Either way, I got to meet Winnie (I mean Danica)!

The Grammys

While touring in Australia with our first record, our manager received a phone call from someone from the Grammy Association and called us into the hotel lobby for a band meeting. We were aware that we were nominated for a few awards that year (2012), but what we were about to find out is that we had been asked if we would be willing to perform with The Beach Boys at the Grammys. We said nothing, but all our faces communicated something like "What the heck is going on?" The Beach Boys, that's right *The Beach Boys*, just asked us to perform with them at the Grammys. We of course said "yes." This request was especially profound for Foster as The Beach Boys and Brian Wilson were a massive influence on his musical journey. Another wild anecdote was that The Beach Boys actually went to my dad's high school. They were a couple of years ahead of him and he remembers the band forming. They returned from their tour at the time to play my dad's senior prom. Pretty wild. The Beach Boys' iconic songs and legendary harmonies were very much a part of my childhood, and our collective respect for them ran deep.

When we got back to LA, a rehearsal was set up for us and The Beach Boys in Burbank, California. As I approached the rehearsal space, I began to hear the low-end frequencies reverberating through the walls. It was getting real. The door flung open and there were The Beach Boys, mid-song and in all their glory.

Vocalist and band cofounder, Mike Love, initially waved us in, calling, "Oh, hey!" Oh hey... Mike. We shook hands with everybody and got acquainted with the rest of the band. Pretty quickly, we pulled out our instruments and slotted in with their team to run our songs a handful of times. Things just clicked. It was equally awesome as it was unbelievable.

After the handful of hours we found to learn the songs and practice while we were still on the road, and the one in-town rehearsal, it seemed like we suddenly found ourselves walking offstage following our dress rehearsal at Staples Center (the host venue for the Grammys). I was heading to the greenroom with Rebecca through the wide corridors under the arena when she tugged on my shirt. "Hey, we just passed Paul McCartney." "You're kidding," I gasped. "You should go meet him," she replied. *Yes. Yes, I should.*

Immediately, I turned around to clue the rest of our band in on the fact that Sir Paul McCartney was behind us. I couldn't believe what I was seeing: Paul seemed to be mutually making a beeline for me. He reached out to shake my hand. "Hey, are you guys Foster the People?" he asked with all the scouse charm in the world. "I was hearing you from backstage and thought it was the Beach Boys. I was shocked when somebody told me it was you guys. It sounded amazing." Paul McCartney notoriously doesn't take photos with people but that day he asked us to take a picture with him.

It's a mind-boggling experience to come off the stage performing with The Beach Boys and to be found backstage by Paul McCartney, not only one of my favorite bass players, but one of the four humans directly responsible for my love of music. I walked back to the greenroom asking, "Did that really just happen?"

We didn't have time to take it all in because we were then ushered straight to a waiting helicopter! Elon Musk had asked us to play at his pre-Grammy party and the only way we could make it work based on the tight schedule was to be transported by helicopter. Elon obliged. Crazy, I know!

Rebecca and I slept at home that night in our little Manhattan Beach apartment. It was a stark contrast to the extraordinary day we had just had. We were able to take a beat and just be a normal married couple for a few hours before returning to Staples Center the next day.

Walking the red carpet felt like an eternity of camera flashes, handshakes, and interviews before we were filed into the auditorium to take our seats. Midway through the evening, our handlers came and pulled us out of the crowd to rush us backstage to change into our show clothes. Behind the scenes it was chaotic. There was an army of people with headsets all communicating at a million miles per hour. There were so many moving parts and people being shuffled that I felt like we were in the middle of a small tornado. Somewhere amidst the chaos, I threw on my bass and we were whisked to side stage. The lights went dark. We took our positions. And with the return of the lights, we were live.

The performance went even better than we'd practiced, and we felt like we were living in a dream. It was as if we could wake up any moment and discover this wasn't our real life. But it was. And while winning a Grammy that night would have been crazy, God was about to hand Rebecca and I something even more grand than anything that experience could have offered me. To this day, this was the greatest gift I could ever receive ...

Rebecca

Our early years of marriage were so redemptive and beautiful. My dreams of married life had finally come true! It was such a delight to not be alone in anything anymore. Joys and challenges, highs and lows were all shared and my heart felt so much lighter. It's like my years of loneliness were being restored. God had been so good—I had been found by true love.

The first Foster the People album was a big favorite of mine, so it was amazing when just a few weeks after our wedding, Cubbie and I headed out on the *Torches* tour. It was a delight to travel the world with Cub and watch from the sound desk night after night, so proud of my man! I appreciate that God had given me, through my life experiences, the ability to understand Cubbie's music journey and support him in the challenges of the spotlight. The mainstream music world that he was living in, and the Christian music life I experienced, were so similar that I had played some of the same venues years before. Truly, God had prepared us for each other, and it was beautiful to experience all this together.

Pretty soon after marriage, I knew the time had come for me to finish out in music, as I wanted to be "all in" on this most prized dream of married life that I was now living. When I finished out the shows I'd committed to and retired quietly from music in 2012, I strongly felt like God was asking me to rest. I even felt that God had specifically called me to a certain time frame for this restoration: six months. There would be no shows, no projects, no writing, no "achieving" anything. Slowly but surely, I began pulling out of performance mode. Instead, I saw friends. I went to the beach. I watched a ton of episodes of *Everybody Loves Raymond* and really, truly laughed for the first time in a while. For a season, I needed to not be responsible for anyone or anything (outside of the joy of caring for my husband!), and it was the deep, soul rest that I so desperately longed for.

While I had always dreamed of building a family, I was okay with us not trying to get pregnant right away. I needed to heal from music burnout. But as I neared the end of my half-year reset, some friends of mine miscarried. The reality of my age and the limited fertility that came with it started to sink in. I was already thirty-five and not getting any younger. Suddenly, I realized that I was ready to try to conceive and I really wanted to be pregnant. It was time, if God would allow it, for me to leave my resting place and start preparing for a child.

The sweetest gift was that God allowed us to conceive almost immediately. I feel quite sure that God prompting me to rest was the reason I fell pregnant right away. I was so thankful! As I stared down at that first positive pregnancy test, extreme joy and excitement coursed through my heart while the question *How is this real?* floated through my mind. We were going to have a baby!

To surprise Cubbie, I made a plan. I scheduled a doctor's appointment and asked for an early ultrasound picture. I kept my surprise a secret until I was holding a little black-and-white ultrasound photo of our child, just a tiny, beautiful little peanut! I presented the photo in a white frame. As Cubbie lifted it out of the gift bag, it took him a moment to register exactly what he was holding. When it finally hit him that this was the first picture of his first child, his eyes lit up. Cubbie was going to be a dad and he was ecstatic!

For our first child, we decided to wait to find out the gender. There are so few surprises left for us as adults, and we wanted to experience all the awe and wonder that we could at the birth of this tiny human. We spent nine months dreaming of who they could be and chose two baby names, one for a boy and one for a girl. *What would the beautiful child God was knitting together in my womb be like?*

Way before I needed them, I started shopping for maternity clothes. I'd browse dreamily through baby stores, buying little things for our growing child. In one store, I even found a five-year diary where I could journal about our baby's life just like my own mom did for me in my "pink book." I picked up books about raising kids and started poring through *Baby Wise* and *Happiest Baby on the Block*.

I was thirty-six throughout my first pregnancy and it was always funny to me that all over my paperwork at my doctor visits was the word "geriatric," like I was a little old lady. But I felt strong and had a great pregnancy. Up until six days past our due date, I was dancing my heart out in my Zumba classes at LA Fitness. My instructor was worried I was going to have the baby right there on the gym floor! Thankfully, I didn't, and our baby stayed put until eight days past their due date when, at around five o'clock in the morning, we grabbed our bags and headed to the hospital for an induction. As we started walking into the maternity ward, it hit me. This is real! We're actually about to have a baby!

Hours later, as the newest member of our family entered the world, Cubbie made a profound announcement ... "It's a girl!!" God had given us a daughter! We gave her a unique name with special meaning, Gemma Elena Fink. "Gemma," which means "precious gem," and her middle name, "Elena," from my mom's name "Helen," which means "shining light." Holding Gemma to my chest, our hearts melted, and we both wept. We had entered a glorious and long-awaited new season of life!

Cubbie

From early on, I knew I wanted to be a husband one day and eventually, a father. I've always loved kids. Even as I aged past the kid table at dinner parties, I found myself skipping out on the adult conversation to laugh and have a good time with the youngest guests.

Beyond genuine care for children, I've also always been fascinated by the unique beauty of innocence and had a desire to protect that for kids. I never wanted to see any child ever robbed of their shameless freedom. When reading *Catcher in the Rye* in high school, I identified with Holden Caulfield, who (spoiler alert), as the narrator of the novel, has been telling his life story from the couch of his psychologist. He processes the vision he had of himself standing in a rye field bordered by cliffs, and his desire to protect the playing children. It's a metaphor of him being the "Catcher in the Rye," catching the kids before they fall off the edge, into loss of innocence. I've always felt led to care for children and point them in the right direction—as both a mentor and a defender.

When I asked Rebecca's dad for his blessing to marry her (remember how that conversation went?), he told me I needed to be prepared to start having children immediately. If that's what Rebecca wanted to do, it didn't scare me at all. Bring on the kids, baby! Rebecca was the one to pump the brakes on that conversation after we first got married. She had a strong desire to heal and lay a solid foundation in our marriage before we introduced a child into the mix, which I was—and still am—very grateful for. We were able to take our time and get to know who we were as a couple before we had to figure out who we were again as parents.

Around the time we hit the half year mark of Rebecca's season of rest, two unique things happened. The first occurred sitting on a flight back to LA. As I looked out my window over the sprawling city below, I remember having the distinct feeling that LA suddenly didn't feel like home anymore. It seemed crazy to admit because I had previously felt so connected and called to the city. But in that moment, I felt released by the Lord and my mind opened to the possibility of a new home on the horizon. Secondly, Rebecca felt ready to start having the "let's have a baby" conversation.

After several discussions and a good bit of time in prayer, we felt the Lord directing our sights to San Diego. It honestly wasn't a very challenging transition to consider. I had grown up there (my parents still lived there), and Rebecca already loved the area because it was where she first landed when she came to California from Nashville. It seemed to be a very natural fit and a significantly better place to raise a family. We quickly found a house a short drive to both my parents and the beach, and like so many young married couples in training for child rearing, we got a dog.

After a few months of settling into our new life rhythm in San Diego, I returned home and was greeted by Rebecca holding a present. Upon opening the gift, I saw a fuzzy black-and-white photo. Staring at it for a moment, my brain started piecing together that this was an ultrasound picture. That little speck was a human that Rebecca and I had created. We were going to be parents!

Band Life

Foster the People had its fair share of internal ups and downs. Even with the best set of circumstances, band life is not easy. I've often heard it referred to as a forced family, with "family life" lived out in the midst of strong opinions, very tight quarters, navigating the vulnerabilities that come with creativity at the core of your profession, all while the world and all its temptations are continuously offered on a silver platter. The clichés are real, and the unfortunate reality is that that world is rife with the pitfalls of pride and addiction. To put it simply, it's hard.

All the typical challenges of being a band are compounded when fame maneuvers its way into the picture. There seems to be a universal allure to fame, but I have come to the firm belief that people were not designed to be famous. Fame, in many ways, scratches the darkest itch of our humanity. One of the first temptations in the garden was an offer to be "like" God. It's hard to not feel god-like when you have the attention and adoration of the world, whether the connection to that world is played out from a stage, big screen, or even a social media platform. Our souls simply cannot bear the weight of worship, and I witnessed firsthand the crushing effect of attempting to receive the glory that can only be carried by the Creator of the universe. It makes sense that so many people in that position turn to vices to help them cope with the overwhelming weight of simultaneously wrestling with the loneliness of being "known" by the world but not truly known by anyone.

Fortunately, I saw this reality very early. The years I lived on mission in South Africa afforded me the insight to never buy into the inherent lie tucked away in the attraction to fame, and the trappings that so commonly come along with it. My identity was, and still is, found complete in my sonship from God the Father, regardless of how many people knew my name or what I did for a living. I am also eternally grateful for the unwavering strength and ever-grounding presence that Rebecca provided me during that season.

While the band found itself in a rough spot by the end of our first album cycle, we took a bit of downtime to recalibrate. With a new approach to internal health, and some fresh vision and inspiration, we collectively moved toward the decision to make a new album. As we worked on the record, I commuted back and forth from San Diego to LA, sometimes having to spend almost the entire work week in the city. But, I got to come home to a refuge of Rebecca in her happy place, where she had dreamed about being since she was a young girl, home-making and mothering our child—before she was even placed into our arms. I, too, was beginning to respond more like a father, before I even realized it.

For our album release party, just a few weeks before our baby was born, we played a show at the base of a huge building in downtown LA. We commissioned an artist to paint our album artwork on the side of the building, which served as a twenty-story-tall backdrop to the show. The afternoon preceding the show, we thought it would be cool to get a picture of the band sitting on the edge of the roof with our legs dangling out over the mural. In years past, I wouldn't have thought twice about doing something like that. I'd spent a lot of time cliff jumping, skydiving, and bungee jumping, and I'd never had even a semblance of a fear of heights.

But suddenly, looking over the edge at the parking lot roughly two hundred feet below, I was paralyzed with fear. I couldn't seem to muster the strength to hoist myself up onto the cinder block wall and transfer my feet from the security of the roof and suspend them midair over the side of the building. I don't think I was able to put words or rational thoughts around it at the time, but I believe that response was a strong sense of paternal instinct kicking in. Somehow, I pushed through my fear and joined the boys on that very narrow wall. We got the shot, and everyone survived.

That was the first thing that really surprised me about becoming a father: a visceral reaction to stay alive, because my life was no longer just my own. I was a part of bringing a child into the world, and I needed to be around to protect her.

Baby Girl

While I was completely at peace and excited about waiting to find out the gender of our baby, my underlying assumption was that we would have a boy.

I'm a boy, and I was born first in my family, so of course that meant we would have a boy first too. *Logic.* The moment I got my first glimpse of our daughter, my heart utterly melted into thoughts of *I have a girl! I'm a father to a little girl!* Being undeniably clear that our baby was indeed female, I leaned over to tell Rebecca, but right before I said anything, I took one more quick look to double confirm. *Yup, definitely a girl.* And then I leaned back to the mother of my daughter to deliver the great news, breaking down before I could finish getting the words out of my mouth. We both immediately started bawling and hugging, a reaction that I will cherish always.

Countless people told me, "Having a baby is the craziest experience you'll ever have." My expectations for just how wild and wonderful the birth experience would be were very high. Even still, it all completely blew my mind. There's nothing that prepares you for watching your wife carry your child inside of her for nine months, fight through the beauty and pain of labor, to then sit and behold this life that God allowed you to be a part of creating.

Nothing can prepare you for that moment when you become a parent. Additionally, nothing could prepare me for how, when I became a girl dad, two things immediately shifted in me that I didn't anticipate.

The first was when my already protective instincts for children compounded into an intense desire to protect my daughter at all costs. There was such a softness and sweetness I could already see in this little girl's heart, and I would do anything to keep someone from ruining that.

The second was when I transported myself into her future and started thinking about how all boys are buttheads. She could one day date some of those buttheads, and it was up to me to teach her how to guard her heart and set high standards. I wanted to know, understand, and walk with her as deeply as I possibly could. I wanted her to not fall or be hurt by any said buttheads.

First-Time Parenting
Rebecca

Before having Gemma, I had many delightful dreams of what life with a baby would look like. Pushing my sweet little one in a stroller, all dressed up in tiny outfits, presenting our precious child to family and friends. As a little girl, I "played house" with my baby doll, but now I was grown up and it was all REAL! I was so very thankful. There were also parts of parenting that came as a shock. Being the oldest daughter in a family of seven kids, I felt like I had already raised a family, and I went into parenting a little overconfident. I had gleaned so much wisdom from my own mum and dad and I'd had years of opportunities to put caregiving knowledge into practice. Plus, I read during pregnancy what I thought were the important parenting books. I studied hard for this. Parenting was a test I was definitely going to pass.

Pretty quickly into mothering Gemma, I realized my thinking had been a little off. On the parenting test, I wasn't sure I was passing with flying colors after all! No amount of studying can prepare you for knowing how to navigate your own unique child. There are a million ways to parent, and many of the daily decisions hinge on what works for your child and what your spouse believes is important in parenting too. It must be taken moment by moment and season by season, I learned.

In the beginning, Cubbie was gone a lot on tour, so I navigated many decisions alone. I had a hard time nursing Gemma so she was hungry and fussed quite a lot, giving way to not much rest for either one of us. (The child did not want to nap!) All the feeding and sleeping schedules I had read about and planned on implementing went straight out the window. Though instruction can help, I quickly discovered you don't learn parenting from a book; you learn it on the job.

Through my current Focus on the Family podcast *Practice Makes Parent* with Dr. Danny Huerta, we've explored a variety of parenting topics, interviewing experts on everything from discipline to anxiety. As we curate conversations for our audience, I continue to glean wisdom. I love it!! For example, I found out through one of our discussions that it didn't matter so much if I had Gemma on the "perfect" schedule. We can take the pressure off ourselves to always do or say the right things in our relationships with our kids because they learn the most by simply being a part of our family, by our example. Whether our children are babies or teenagers, they absorb how to live by living with us. When we parents realize that little eyes are watching us under a microscope, seeing and imitating us, we can be intimidated. It seems like there's no room to mess up. However, while it's awesome for our children to see us succeed, they also need to see us fail and get back up again. And when we fail them, they need to see us own it, apologize, and resolve the conflict. That's how they, too, learn to make mistakes and grow. We have to give ourselves grace and then extend that same compassion to our spouses as we navigate parenting together.

From the early stages of parenthood, Cubbie and I have been having an ongoing conversation about how extending grace and cultivating our relationship with each other directly affects the overall health of our family. My dad always loved the quote "The best thing a father can do for his kids is to love their mother," and I have applied it to myself as a mum. The best way I can love my kids is to love Cubbie well. Especially when there were tiny children in the house and we were both exhausted, it was easy to slip into functioning more like roommates than spouses. To break the cycle of to-dos, we had to learn to make time for "us" to have regular date nights.

When I say "date night," I don't necessarily mean anything fancy. Sometimes just organizing a sitter and getting out the door in jeans and a T-shirt felt like a massive feat with a small child. Our "date night" was just a focused, intentionally planned time for Cubbie and I to check in with each other. We would ask questions like, "How can I support and love you best right now?" "How's your heart on a scale of one to ten?" It might sound a little cheesy, but I know we both felt cared for in these moments. When we stay connected in our marriage, especially in seasons where there is a lot of tension and busyness, it brings joy and stability to our homes. When parents are on the same page, kids feel grounded and secure too.

I'm so grateful we learned to become adaptive and stay connected early on as parents because these are the skills we used to bind us together when the challenges of life later threatened to pull us apart.

Chapter 10

THE WINTER SEASON

Rebecca

Despite my dreams of becoming a wife and mom coming true, I still dealt with post-burnout anxiety. My mind was having its first real moments to pause and process all that had happened in the story of my life, and counseling was helping me sort through the highs and lows. During that time, my actual dreams were littered with instances of me being called to come out onstage but not being dressed in my stage clothes. The announcer would be saying my name, people were waiting, but I couldn't walk out in my unprepared state. So, I just stayed backstage, listening to my invitation to go sing for the crowd, and freaking out because I wasn't ready. Stress dream after stress dream rolled through my nights.

There were and still are times when Cubbie has to grab me because I'm ramping up with a performance nightmare. He reaches over, calms me down, and reminds me that it's all just a dream. Physically and mentally, these nightmares have felt so real because often, the unprepared, vulnerable, exposed feeling in my shows had been real. At that time in my life, off the stage and out of the lights, I found myself wrestling with my identity and worth. Like never before, questions were surfacing like:

> *Do I have the same value serving at home here with one child as*
> *I did ministering on stages in front of thousands?*
> *When wounds are soul deep, do they leave you with a permanent*
> *emotional limp?*
> *Can I actually trust God to restore me when you can apparently*
> *become depleted while doing His work?*
> *Am I valuable to others even when I'm struggling like this?*

My counselor offered me this wise piece of advice:

> You can sit in a room and not say one thing to the person that you're in the room with, and just your presence alone, who God made you to be, who you *are*, is a gift. You do not have to perform. You don't even have to encourage. You don't have to do anything but sit in that chair and you will be a blessing.

I knew he was right. But just sitting still and doing little didn't feel like it was enough. I didn't know how to move slow or live comparatively "small," even though little is all I felt capable of offering. God was teaching me to "be" instead of "do" and that my value was not in my performance but in who He made me to be and because of His presence in me. I know a lot of moms deal with these kinds of struggles, especially after working outside the home. Our culture does not uphold or honor the role of mothering in the way that it should. I had to learn how to enjoy deep moments of satisfaction in quiet experiences of joy with my daughter and in caring for our home, without the praise and admiration of many. I had to learn to hear God's "Well done!" as I went about my daily duties and to experience His smile as I lived out this new role. I was His daughter—accepted and beloved just as I was.

This lesson of just *being* was a hard one to learn because it put me in a secret place with my sweet baby girl that was so opposite of my formerly "large," public life full of concerts, albums, writing, and ministry. It was such a juxtaposed time. I was delighted to be a mum, and I was doing my dream job, but there were very few cheers for my performance at home. There was no rock show high after rocking my baby to sleep.

There was just a quiet that shouted that I needed to deal with my still aching heart. My soul recognized that my years of ministry had left me with scars, and a big part of me still felt like a shell of my former self.

That's why when Cubbie walked in after a band meeting, I recognized the internal struggle he was displaying in his heavy eyes. His look mirrored my own as I braced myself for the words I knew were coming yet couldn't believe were real.

"It's done."

Leaving the Band
Cubbie

The band had been gracious to try to delay things as much as possible around Gemma's birth, but roughly a week after she was born, I had to head back out for another trip around the globe to support our new record. While a world tour would have been many musicians' dream, I was having quite a hard time leaving my newborn baby girl.

Rebecca and I committed early in our marriage to not go longer than two weeks without seeing each other. While this was challenging at times, and often required some creative travel gymnastics, we made it happen. When days apart would start to feel taxing, knowing I was going to see my beautiful wife again soon pulled me through. At a time we could have drifted apart, our determination to remain connected strengthened our marriage. I would encourage every married touring musician (or anyone who travels consistently for work) to make a similar commitment.

But now with a newborn, and the majority of our touring overseas, it became close to impossible to continue to uphold this commitment. Being away from my wife and our brand-new daughter was incredibly painful. They were magnets pulling me home and I was consistently forced to resist the draw as I traveled, feeling always like I wasn't pointed to my true north.

During a few legs of our US runs, we did our best to have Rebecca and Gemma join me. Having a baby on the bus was not optimal, so we decided to rent an RV to follow behind. My dear friend, and assistant tour manager at the time, and I would take turns driving. It was a lot of long nights after days filled with fulfilling band obligations, playing shows, and often DJing after parties late into the night. Despite the challenges, it was so worth it to have them with me. While the couple runs in the RV were amazing, in the end, I was gone for the better part of eleven months of the first year of Gemma's life.

As exhilarating as it was to step through the doors the Lord had seemingly opened for Foster the People to launch into the global arena, it was incredibly challenging to watch how the rock 'n' roll lifestyle and mindset distorted and eventually eroded the foundation of the band. Maintaining the purpose I thought the band was founded on was becoming less and less of a focal point for the other guys. The world has a crafty way of assuming, and eventually demanding, full focus.

Despite the attempts toward a healthier approach, a few months into the new tour it became clear the band was yet again heading down an all too familiar unhealthy road. It didn't take long for it to completely spiral out of control. Whether voluntarily or by election, I had always assumed a bit of a fatherly role on the road. In fact, one of my band-given nicknames was "Mufasa," the father from *The Lion King*. I had a heart for my bandmates and our crew; they were loved brothers and true family to me. I deeply desired to be an ambassador of Truth and a bearer of Christ's love on the road. But even on that front, I picked up that my attempts to nudge things back toward Truth were becoming less and less appreciated.

Was this worth it? I wasn't so sure anymore. It was becoming harder and harder for me to justify spending that much time away from my wife and brand-new child just for the sake of playing music. Sure, the show was always the thing I looked forward to day in and day out, but I could no longer fully buy into the big picture of what the band was standing for. The foundation of calling I associated with the band was cracked, the mission seemingly evaporated. If I was going to be away from my family, I needed purpose behind it to keep going. I assume my gradual disconnection and withdrawal was felt by the guys. At the end of the day, I was not providing them what they truly desired of me: to be completely and wholeheartedly committed to the band and sold out for the music. I unfortunately lacked the ability to offer an "all in" kind of commitment without true alignment on the purpose behind the music.

We played our final show of that tour in Santa Barbara and wrapped everything up with a party at a big house on the beach. While it was fun, at the same time it was awkward because I could sense there was change in the winds. Something was about to happen.

Sure enough, about a week later, Foster called and said, "Hey, we need to talk." Nothing good ever follows that, right? So I drove up to his place in downtown LA and sat down with him and Pontius. They had made a decision to move on without me.

While tensions had clearly been rising, I still felt completely blindsided. I just never, in a million years, would have anticipated my leaving the band happening like this. We were equal owners, the three of us, and we voted on everything we did as a band. We all had an equal say in every decision. Obviously, two votes beat one. While I tried to fight for my place in the band, there was very little room for discussion. It was just over. One minute, I had a career, the next minute, my feet were knocked clean out from underneath me. Suddenly, a choice that terminated my job and means for providing for my family had been made for me and threw me into a season of complete unknown.

Rebecca was in the kitchen of our house in San Diego when I came through the door and announced, "Well, it's done." With questions of "What do we do now?" and "What is God doing?" floating through the air, Rebecca cut through with clarity. "God's got us. We'll be okay."

Somewhere deep down I knew she was right. We would be okay, but I was rocked with disbelief at our current situation. For me, I also felt a sense of calling and loyalty to the band. We had gone through so much together, making us more like brothers than bandmates. It was hard to wrap my head around the fact that I was being pushed out of something that God seemingly orchestrated.

It was wild to see our years together come to this. How could all the beauty of what God had done with the music and the prophecies about the band that I had seen fulfilled in uncanny detail, be obliterated just like that? While it was impossible to deny what I saw and experienced, I began to question what I heard from the Lord. Did I make that up? After calling into question the last several years, I began asking God, "What am I meant to do now?"

The hardest part of it all wasn't the loss of my position, or the feeling of betrayal, but the fact that my question for God was met with complete and utter silence. I was in an incredibly foreign and unfamiliar territory. At every other major turning point in my life, God had been exponentially clear with me on what I was to do. *Go to South Africa. Head back to college. Study film. LA is the new mission field. Focus on music. Here's the band.* But at that moment, standing at the biggest crossroad of my life, a crossroad that involved not only me but now my wife and one-year-old daughter, God said ... nothing. For the first time in decades, I didn't know what I was meant to do next.

Purpose

My struggles were tied more to my sense of calling than my identity. Sure, the season with the band was fun. It was a blast traveling the world and meeting incredible people while playing music that I loved. I will be forever grateful for those opportunities. But if someone would have asked me, "Who are you?" my answer during that season would not have been, "I am a bass player." I always knew that who I was reached beyond what I do.

But this is where things got complicated for me. While my identity wasn't wrapped up in the band, I quickly realized it was in some ways tied to a sense of calling attached to music. Just like Rebecca and her voice, for years I saw music as the vehicle God used to drive out my purpose. All of a sudden, I didn't have a vehicle. Now I seemingly had nothing to drive me forward. I wrestled through thoughts that I had completely blown it for my growing family and myself. In my gut, I knew I couldn't have saved the situation, yet I still carried the weight of so much guilt. I started to buy into a false doctrine I had never believed before. I thought I had somehow stepped out of God's will for my life and into some weird wasteland where He couldn't use me anymore.

I was grasping for what was next and not finding any handles as I fell into a state of depression. The darkness that seeped into my mind contrasted starkly to the bright excitement of our lives. Our daughter Gemma was healthy and we had just started transforming our San Diego fixer-upper in a part of town just a walk or bike ride away from the beach, coffee shops, and my favorite Mexican restaurants. Externally, our life looked "perfect," but internally, I was off kilter and in total disarray.

Trauma Responses

I began to notice that my general responses to situations and conversations were not congruent with the things I was reacting to. The littlest things seemed huge and would completely throw me off, for hours, days, or even weeks. We were obviously navigating a challenging season, but what I realized was that these overreactions were evidence of something much deeper beneath the surface.

The best analogy I can offer is this: If you reach out and touch someone's forearm, a natural response from the person being touched would be to look down and ask, "Why are you touching my arm?" They might slowly move their arm away from your hand. But if that arm has a gaping wound, and you put your finger into that wound, the reaction is a lot more volatile. They might jump back and yell, "Wow, why did you do that?" The same touch could cause different reactions based on the condition of the receiver. I was the one with the gaping wound, and the most challenging part, which only created more shame in me, was that Rebecca was the one who often received the full emotional brunt of these reactions.

In prior years, I was always incredibly confident and secure. Suddenly, my confidence was completely shot, and my security was thrown into subjection. I didn't know who I was anymore, and I kept blaming myself for everything. I never viewed myself as a victim in my situation, but I did think I deserved the punches I kept throwing at myself. Hit after hit, I'd replay scenarios and conversations wondering how I could have done things differently so that none of this would have happened. *If I would have reached out here, or said something there, would I still have my job?* Eventually, I knocked myself deep enough into a hole of self-sabotaging shame that I didn't know how to get myself out.

With Rebecca's encouragement, I started to see a counselor in San Diego. While I felt like my life was in shambles, we were also in the middle of renovating our new home and living in it during the renovation. That's enough to drive anyone crazy. Just like my actual house wasn't a place of peace and sanctuary, my counselor helped me understand there were open holes in my mental and emotional foundation that also needed repair. As we started to pull back the layers of my life to see what was under the rubble, I discovered there was so much more than I had ever known. The missing memories in my life were linked to some sort of trauma so severe that it had caused a mental block in my childhood. There were wounds I had somehow managed to cover for decades that were now being poked and prodded at. I wanted to ignore the pain, but I could see how my actions and overreactions were affecting my wife and daughter. I had to find healing. And I had to find a job.

Rebecca

As an adventurous couple, we had always been rewarded for risk. But suddenly, it seemed like a lot of what we had gambled on, we had lost. So, we pulled back and thought the answer to our problems was to not take bold steps of faith anymore. What if we lived "safe" for a season and chilled out and stayed close to home? We had been wounded and we needed to heal. No more risks; let's just rest. Let's be "normal" (whatever that means). And that dialed-back life, where we produced little fruit and reaped little harvest, marked our barren winter season.

Sometimes the ground needs to lay bare. The soil of our lives needs to rest so it can produce harvest again. Emotionally, this is what had to happen for us. We also had to ask ourselves hard questions. *Outside of all we had done and accomplished in our lives, who were we again?*

It was a full-blown retreat. The troops had been advancing and things were exploding, so we pulled back to seek a haven, a quiet place to land. I was still learning how to be a mum while also trying to carry the weight of everything going on with Cubbie. I remember wanting to authentically encourage him and give support, but I was struggling to stay afloat myself. Truthfully, I felt shocked and quite afraid.

Subconsciously it was as if I had bought into this idea that if we're faithful to God and committed to holiness, if we check off all the right Christian boxes, then surely blessing and protection from great life losses will follow. There was an entitlement where I thought we were worthy to be exempt from intense pain because we had both fought to be "faithful in ministry." Cubbie was so devoted and full of integrity. I thought that should have earned him some protection from this kind of pain.

I learned the hard way—through experiencing it firsthand and seeing my loved one suffer without being able to fix things for him—that life doesn't always add up according to our understanding. It seems obvious now because Jesus Himself, perfect and sinless, was not exempt from the challenges and pain of life in this world. In hindsight, I've come to realize that my faith had become transactional in nature, which is humbling to admit. We can't trade our works for blessings. We've since learned to trust God is at work in all our situations, the easy and the hard. We cannot earn His love or any blessings in this life—it's all His grace and mercy. "Every good and perfect gift is from above, coming down from the Father" (James 1:17).

My fears and questioning were only compounded when we decided to start trying for another baby shortly after Cubbie's departure from the band and I miscarried. We tried again and I found out I was pregnant once more in the fall of 2016. I wanted to use Cubbie's birthday in early October to share the news. Gemma and I gave him a few gifts but saved the final one, a positive digital pregnancy test as the baby announcement. It felt exciting and vulnerable at the same time. I kept asking myself, *Is this one really going to stick?* I was as hopeful as any mom could be giving my husband this gift, but I was also scared that it would again be taken away from us. Cubbie celebrated in a big way with Gemma and I, but I recognized a slightly worried look in his eyes that I'm sure matched my own. It is so incredibly hard to be thrilled and yet terrified.

A couple of weeks later, we traveled to Australia for a few ministry events. At that time, I was almost never performing. This was one of the few singing opportunities I accepted in that winter season, mostly because it got our little family back to Australia. While we were there, I started bleeding. I knew it could be implantation bleeding and not actually a miscarriage, so I tried to stay positive. But my hope decreased as the bleeding became heavier.

In a photo from the trip, I'm standing on the stage in front of a venue I had been to with my dad as a child, proud to now be the one singing there. It's hard to look back at pictures of me from that time in Sydney, realizing what was happening. That woman standing in that photo is holding so much gain and loss in the same moment.

We came home and it was confirmed that I had miscarried again. On top of everything else, now my body was failing me a second time. It was not doing what I thought I knew it was created to do: mother multiple children. We knew we weren't meant to be a one child family. For many years, I said often from the stage that I wanted seven to ten kids! But now we couldn't seem to conceive a second child, let alone more. Lifelong dreams were being dashed. We rode waves of grief as we were already trying to navigate the tumultuous waters of finding a new source of income, healing from trauma, and slowly rediscovering our identity in Christ. *If God is the giver of Life, why would He take so much away?*

Cubbie

Rebecca was already hurting for me because of everything I was walking through from parting ways with the band and the general upheaval that ensued.

Amid all this, we decided to start trying for another child. We originally had talked about having three, four, or even five kids. While it happened relatively easily with Gemma, getting pregnant was proving to be a bit more challenging the second time around. Finally, after several months of trying, we were holding a positive pregnancy test.

The hope of this new baby was a little bright spot in our lives that we met with so much joy. A couple months into the pregnancy, we went to an ultrasound appointment, excited to hear the baby's heartbeat, and instead we were met with silence. *Silence.* Why? Why was everything stained with silence in this season? We were shocked as the weight of reality began to close in on us in that little patient room. We, too, became silent, and quiet tears slowly streamed down Rebecca's face.

As the months passed, we continued to try to grow our family. With our next positive pregnancy test, we were excited but this time a bit more reserved. Like a replay of the months before, we walked into the ultrasound room only to again hear no heartbeat. *Silence.*

I had heard stories of couples miscarrying, and though I knew it was incredibly sad, I never really understood the weight of it. It's so much heavier and harder than I could have ever anticipated because the moment you realize there's life inside of your wife's body that you helped create, there's an automatic connection. I know it runs much deeper for a woman, but even as a father, there is an automatic kindredness we have with our child in the womb. It's heart wrenching the moment you know, no matter what phase of the pregnancy, that your unborn child has died. You never get to meet them. Hold their hand. Guide them through life.

Our miscarriages were just more wood on the fire of this raging season of pain. Everything started compounding on top of each other; the silence, lack of direction, obliteration of dreams, confusion around callings, unearthing childhood trauma, and the actual loss of life in our family felt like a bonfire twenty stories high that we, no matter what we threw at it, couldn't put out.

When I was in South Africa years before, my mom mentioned to me that she was getting some testing done. She had been showing possible signs of multiple sclerosis. Her results eventually came back positive, but she sought treatment, and we all prayed for almost a decade for a miracle. Now that we lived close to my parents, I was daily witness to my mom's dwindling ability to move. She transferred from a cane to a walker, and eventually from the walker to a wheelchair. She got to the point that she was unable to do much of anything on her own, and my dad lovingly assumed the role of full-time caretaker.

I deeply love my mom, and so much of who I am I attribute to her. She was the one who first introduced me to art. Growing up, she was always doodling, painting, or working with clay. On nearly a daily basis she would work up some form of an art or craft project for my sister and I to enjoy and express ourselves through. She was a great photographer, and it was by her influence that I fell in love with the world as seen through a viewfinder. It was this passion that eventually evolved into my pursuit of film. Now, those hands that had carried me and crafted so much, could hold nothing. I was watching my mom deteriorate from the disease that would eventually take her life. All the while, I was asking God for help and being met with more silence.

Rebecca and I were both so exhausted and overwhelmed from our hurt and confusion that we hardly had anything to offer each other. Neither one of us could be "the strong one" in our relationship to shoulder the weight and get us through. We were depleted and weak as we tried to sort through the layers of hard that just kept being thrown on top of our already very hard season.

The Sixth Love Language
Rebecca

In our winter season, Cubbie and I came to know suffering on a whole new level because we were mourning our losses at the same time. He couldn't carry me through my burnout and grief, and I couldn't equip him to walk through his healing from trauma. As a married couple who were each carrying heavy burdens, the best way we learned to provide support to each other, beyond going to God together in prayer, was to ask questions.

During this time, our marriage greatly benefited from what I coined a "sixth love language." "Love languages" are terminology commonly referred to from Gary Chapman's book *The 5 Love Languages*, which we read when we first got married. It's an incredibly insightful, faith-based book that couples can use as a tool to understand how their spouses best experience and understand love. The languages are words of affirmation, receiving gifts, quality time, acts of service, and physical touch. I think in times of great suffering there is a sixth "love language" that both partners can benefit from—curiosity.

Genuinely asking someone, "How are you *really* doing?" is one of the most loving things we can do, especially for our spouses. This loving curiosity applies to all our relationships because it displays that we genuinely want to know someone's heart. Curiosity is evidence that you care. So, when the hurt is too great, don't withdraw, try to connect through curiosity. Ask questions like: *How is everything going today? How's your heart? How are you, really? How can I support you right now?* Hold space for them to respond. Simply listen. Be there with them in the pain if they have no words. Because, when you can't give anything else, a listening ear and receiving presence is enough and will keep you connected as a couple in a season where it's tempting to withdraw.

Some of my most precious times with God have been going on walks in nature and talking to Him. There are times when I'm simply tuning into the presence of God that I feel He's a smiling friend, kindly but curiously asking, "How are you *really* doing? Tell Me everything." Obviously, God knows all the aspects of my heart and how I'm feeling, but I think these moments of connection when He's asking me to share, build intimacy. He wants me to know He cares, that He rejoices over me "with gladness" and that I can trust Him with my whole heart (Zeph. 3:17 ESV). God is curious about His children.

Whether we're married or single, I believe this idea of curiosity extends not only into our walk with God, but also to how we connect in all our relationships, including our parenting. For example, I've learned that children see evidence that we care when we show we want to know them. When we hear them out, hold the things they're worried about, and celebrate in their joys, it's powerful. Dr. Anthony P. Witham famously said, "Kids spell love T-I-M-E." To show our kids our love, we give them our time. Getting to know our kids—by staying curious about them—is how we build a solid relationship.

While it's important that we stay curious about the people we care about, it's easy in hardship to go into survival mode and self-preserve. We tend to think our spouse, friend, or family member can figure this out for themselves while we're figuring things out for ourselves, but a posture of curiosity allows us to suffer well together. While we can't fix everything, we can know each other's heartache and hold space for all the mixed emotions that come from being people who are experiencing deep pain.

The greatest example I know of how to seek joy together amid sorrow is shown in the film about the life of C. S. Lewis, *Shadowlands*. In the movie, Lewis's wife has cancer and he's terrified of losing her. They share an amazing moment running through a beautiful field in the rain, but you can sense an undertone of sadness to their overwhelming joy because of her illness and the uncertainty of their future. Lewis reflects later in his life about that moment, "Twice in life I've been given the choice: as a boy and as a man. The boy chose safety, the man chooses suffering. The pain now is part of the happiness then."[7]

For so much of my life, I thought pain and joy were mutually exclusive; you couldn't hold both in your heart at the same time. But as I've gotten older, I've noticed there is something beautiful about the highs and lows intertwining. There was something so sweet about Cubbie holding me as I cried while I was simultaneously holding him. Even there in the tears was the joy we shared that we weren't alone. In walking through this together, we were growing closer. Instead of fighting against the pain, our curiosity allowed us to slowly make peace with it. We sought God and each other not only for relief but for comfort right there in the messy middle.

And if you can't find words, offer a physical touch. By just reaching out towards one another, we can tangibly become each other's safe place when our speech can't offer it. So often when Cubbie and I embrace, we audibly sigh because it brings solace. Then our kids squeeze themselves into the middle of our hug knowing they belong in that circle of love and security. If life is complicated, keep it simple. Ask questions, hold each other, and always look toward Jesus.

Jesus was "a man of sorrows, and familiar with suffering" (Isa. 53:3). He's not intimidated by our problems, anger, sorrow, grief, and questions. His ministry here on earth was a complete mix of sorrow and joy, life and death. The mix is important because "suffering produces endurance, and endurance produces character, and character produces hope, and hope does not put us to shame, because God's love has been poured into our hearts through the Holy Spirit who has been given to us" (Rom. 5:3–5 ESV).

When pain sweeps in and threatens to knock you off your feet, stand firm in your care for others and faith in Christ by remaining curious and openhearted. Ask the questions and know that it's okay to not have all the answers. Create space for God to respond and slowly, but surely, you'll discover that your love and His love will get you through. You will hear His voice again.

Cubbie

Here is a truth I eventually arrived at in this season: when you don't know what to do, do what worked before and let God take it from there. I suppose I am someone people would consider a "creative type." The thing that might make me a bit different from a typical artist is that the practical side of my nature is just about as strong as the creative side. In this new season of trying to figure out what was next, having gone somewhat neglected for far too long, my practical side was definitely screaming for attention. A big part of me just wanted something that made sense. In the creative world, very little makes practical sense: A plus B generally never equals C, and I was in a place where I desperately wanted C to be the sum of A and B. Give me some nails and a pile of wood and let me build something! Give me a plot of dirt and some seeds and let me grow something! So, naturally, I explored and dreamed about everything from house flipping to wheat farming, and a good few things in between. After months of traversing and continually being met with an obvious lack of peace, my mind and heart led me back to where everything started for me ... youth ministry.

I've always had a heart for young people and decided to take a leap back to my roots by accepting a job as an interim student pastor. As if my spirit was stepping through the door back into the Dutch Reformed Church, my passion for seeing students encounter the Holy Spirit immediately rekindled. Before, I was only a year or two older than the students I worked with. Now, because of the wisdom afforded by my life experiences, I felt like I had more to offer as a mentor rather than just a friend. I was reminded how much of our lives and legacy of faith are built in those four to five formative years of high school into early college.

As fulfilling as the ministry was, and as much as I absolutely loved my year with those students, it lacked the deep-seated sense of peace and calling that I was doing exactly what I was put on the planet to do. This "lack" was perplexing to me and I kept asking God, "How much more can I do for the kingdom than serve the Church and the next generation of Christian leaders?" It was my heart to continue to serve until I received a clear answer that it was time to move on.

Chapter 11

SPRING BEGINS

Rebecca

In 2017, we were six years into our marriage and I was about to turn forty when we decided to say "yes" to an upcoming show in Alaska. I still had offers coming in pretty regularly to my booking agency, but they knew in that season that the answer was a default "no." However, when The WayFM radio network asked me and my brothers Joel and Luke to sing on a cruise to Alaska, it actually seemed like a golden opportunity to take a much-needed vacation with the entire Smallbone clan. Truthfully, Cubbie and I needed the change in scenery, and we were hopeful that a break would be a healthy choice for us.

I wish I could say that my years of rest, at home with Gemma and spending simple times as a family, healed the anxiety I had around singing. I want to tell you that I seized this opportunity with excitement and confidence. But,

I didn't. I still had major vocal issues. When I retired, I never wanted to pick performing back up again and I felt peaceful about ending that chapter and starting a new one. I just didn't sing anymore, so accepting this offer was a huge deal for me. I was fearful as I thought about stepping back onstage at one of the big cruise ship auditoriums. It was as if that stage was an arena where I was about to face a miracle or a monster. I wasn't sure which I was going to get.

Despite being teary right before sound check, my voice held up during the worship set I carried in that auditorium full of about eight hundred cruise goers. In between songs, I felt that God wanted me to be real about the season I was in. In my shows in the past, I thought I needed to wrap everything up in a bow and share about things after God had already put it all back together. But here was God asking me to be vulnerable and raw about the here and now, to talk about the winter season in our souls, while it was still happening.

"Hey, we're in this season that feels really different to anything we've been through before," the transparent story began to flow from my heart through my words. "We've had two miscarriages. Our family is facing a lot of unknowns and pain and we're trying to open our hands and trust God in the middle of it. We're trying to trust His goodness and faithfulness even when we don't see how this is going to turn out." In between the tears that were streaming down my face, I noticed there was almost no dry eye in the room. I could hear people sniffling and being moved by the Holy Spirit too.

In that powerful moment, something shifted in my soul. As if my tears were the rain in the cloud that had been hovering over my life, suffocating my voice, I felt the release of them allow the sun to shine again. I could see God's light like I used to in my shows before pain and fear had overshadowed my ability to fully sense His nearness. God and I were again connected through music, and I felt His joy and pleasure in me as I continued to lead that room full of people in worship. I realized that I had deeply missed the connection with Jesus and dependence that I have on the Holy Spirit when I sing. My heart had turned a corner.

With this huge pivot, my history shifted in my mind, taking on a new perspective. Floating on a ship in an Alaskan sea, I could suddenly see how God had been there loving me through every dark, dormant moment of my life. Music was no longer the scary monster it had been, it was the vehicle God used for my miracle. The music in my heart was returning!

As I exited the stage, I saw Joel and his wife, Moriah, in the greenroom and said, "I'm not sure that I know the fullness yet of what just happened out there onstage, but I think God just called me back to music." That turned out to be the most instantaneously transformative experience of my life. The winter was thawing and spring had begun ...

Cubbie

As the date for the cruise came closer, I could tell Rebecca's fear and anxiety were stirring up again. Just singing a couple of songs was incredibly overwhelming. While neither one of us were clearly in a great place, we decided to try to make the best of it. The church had offered to convert my interim role into a full-time position. I told them I needed some time to think and pray about it, and an Alaskan cruise seemed like the perfect opportunity to decide if I should take the job. I boarded the ship with a direct prayer for an answer.

The first morning as we sailed through the Canadian Isles, making our way north to Alaska, I sat on our bed in our stateroom with the curtains open, enjoying the views. Bible open and in prayer, I was observing the majestic mountains jetting up out of the ocean toward the sky when something gave me pause. Did I hear something? The Voice. The silence was broken with one word. "Running."

Running? What, Lord? I know I've put on a few pounds, but do I need to go exercise or something? This word made zero sense initially, but as I sat with it, I began to see a picture of myself running away from music, running away from film, and running away from the core of what I was made to do ... create. In that season I struggled to listen to music, kept all artistic endeavors at arm's length, and played it safe in a job that by its very nature was beautiful, but kept me from what I was created to do.

I realized how scared I had been to venture back into the artistic world. I didn't want to get hurt again. Sitting in the weight of that revelation, I knew I needed to stop and make a one hundred and eighty degree turn from my life of practicality and comfort and return to the arts, film, and music again. I just needed to stop running. It was like God kindly slapped me on the back of the head and said, "Dude, you're running from the thing I created you to do. You need to turn around and start walking back."

Running. I allowed myself to fully accept the meaning of that word. A piece of me had been missing and with my small hint of willingness to leap back into all God had for me, I was beginning to see everything puzzling in my life come back together. Along with the newfound clarity came an overwhelming amount of peace. My fears were met with a sense of security that God was going to be with me despite the pain that was still very real, and the trauma that lurked in the back of my mind. Finally, something felt right. I was overwhelmed with inspiration, vision, and direction, things I hadn't had in years. I felt purpose again.

Suddenly the road opened before me. I could see where and how I needed to walk to get where God wanted me to go. I was excited again about film and music. It was radical. This was the birth of a new dream and vision that changed the direction for my life and our family.

When we got off the ship and broke down all that the Lord had revealed over the course of the last few days, Rebecca and I instantly realized the cruise was a massive turning point for both of us. God's undeniable direction in our lives led us to discuss a move that had been completely off the table until that moment when all arrows began to point in one direction—Nashville, Tennessee.

TO BE KNOWN

Rebecca

It's so hard to allow ourselves to believe, through Jesus, that our pain carries purpose when we're undergoing great suffering or grief. When you're facing a winter season in life, and you hear, "God's going to use this! He's good so it's not over until it's good!" you know they're right, but you almost want to scream back, "So what! This hurts so bad right now. Why would He allow it?"

Here's what Cubbie and I have learned from weathering our winter season—God truly, intimately knows us. I love how sweetly Jeremiah 1:5 states, "Before I formed you in the womb I knew you, before you were born I set you apart." Before we even breathed our first breath, God's mind and heart were fixed on us. It's wild to think about. But in every season, in our barren winters and most productive summers, when I was a confident kid and later when I was wrecked by fear, on stages and in secret places, God has known me in full and still receives me, wants me, and chooses me as His daughter.

God knows us and there's nothing you or I can do to change that. While it's a little unnerving that the perfect God of the universe is well acquainted with our every flaw, the desire of the human heart is to be known because that's how we know we're loved. **We can't be fully loved without being fully known.**

This too is why, as we've discovered, a cherished marriage gets so much better through the years. There's more intimacy because you've seen each other's best character traits and worst flaws yet chosen your spouse anyway. There's more grace because you've gone through the highs and lows of life together.

The cruise was this pivotal moment where I heard God saying, "I see you, daughter. I see the pain you've walked through in your life. I'm healing that. I'm redeeming that. And I see this beautiful future for you of new dreams and new joy and restoration. I know those longings of your heart." It's been over seven years since then, and I'm now experiencing thriving ministry. My voice has returned, strengthened, deepened, and grown, as have I. Though life is never perfect and there are still challenges, I'm leaning on the Holy Spirit and seeing Him lead me. And, because I've learned to guard my heart and my schedule, serving through singing is not so costly. It's redemptive.

I often think about the concept of knowing and being known because of being a parent. I want our children to grow up experiencing what it is to truly connect with others and be known themselves. Our culture is so distracted by phones and media that it can prevent us from authentically connecting, which is at the core of truly knowing. Our kids are asking questions but we might not be available to answer them because we're texting someone back instead. Social media is an extremely poor imitation of real relationships yet such a large part of how we relate today that many of us don't know how to connect without it. This causes all kinds of social and emotional problems. Our children will sadly never know a world without social media and cell phones so we must have great wisdom as we navigate the challenge of putting away our screens so we can get face-to-face with our kids.

To make sure our own children are known by us and that they under-stand what it means to be known by God, Cub and I have chosen to do a few simple things. We try our best to not be on our phones much around our kids. We seek to have regular family meals and devotions. We limit screen time. Especially with our oldest child moving into her preteen years, we want to be available for important conversations and questions. We also don't want to load our kids up with a ton of extracurricular activities, not that those are bad things. We just don't want to be constantly shuffling our kids to the next thing they *need* to do. Instead, we want to live more simply than we have in other seasons and not be caught up in the hustle of modern family life. **When it comes to raising a family, sometimes less is more and simpler is better.**

Sometimes we have to slow our lives down, to provide time for our kids to be known and to know us, to have those important moments of connection. Regularly, my middle daughter and I have this connecting conversation right before bed, one that intentionally speaks grace to her:

"Do you know Mommy and Daddy love you?"

"Yes."

"Do you know we love you when you do good things?"

"Yes."

"Do you know we love you when you do wrong things?"

"Yes."

"Who else loves you like that?"

"God does."

"Rest in that love."[8]

As parents, Cubbie and I want to show our children that we love, see, and choose them no matter what, and that God does the same. Because I've experienced being known by God in the middle of my pain, and experienced His rich grace towards me, I'm passionate about my own children grabbing a hold of this concept for themselves.

It's interesting to me that the feature song chosen for the *Unsung Hero* movie is "You Make Everything Beautiful." Ironically, I wrote it in one of the least beautiful seasons of my life. It was part of the album I recorded right before I retired, when the fears surrounding my voice were at their worst. I struggled through every word in the studio, and yet, I sang them because I know they are true. When I performed the song, it always connected with the audience, making me feel the final story had not yet been written when it came to that song.

Thirteen years after it was first released, God brought "You Make Everything Beautiful" to life in a new way through the movie. I speak these lyrics over you

now as you hold joy and grief, light and darkness, hope and disappointment—
all simultaneously. May you feel deeply known by God as you read these words.
And for those of you in "winter," may you find yourself singing amidst suffering
as you believe for your own shift in the seasons:

> *Grant me serenity to accept things*
> *The things I cannot change*
> *Grant me the courage, Lord, to change what I can*
> *Wisdom to know the difference*
> *In my weakness You can shine*
> *In Your strength I can fly*
>
> *And You make everything, everything beautiful*
> *You make everything, everything new*
> *You make everything, everything beautiful*
> *In its time, in Your time*
> *It's beautiful.*[9]

LOVED

Chapter 12

COMING BACK HOME

Cubbie

Pretty much from the moment Rebecca and I got married, her entire family pestered us with the question "So when are you guys moving to Nashville?" To which we would always laugh and say, "It's not gonna happen." Behind those words was the firm belief that it would take an act of God to get us to move there. Having spent most of my life near the beach, I was always horrified by the thought of being landlocked and that far from the ocean. For Rebecca, Nashville represented a painful place from her past, a fishbowl of Christian music from which she had left with no intentions of returning. *Besides, why would we leave our freshly renovated house, mere blocks from the surf in perfect year-round seventy-two-degree sunny San Diego? We were living the dream.*

But a shift happened on the cruise that left a curious question mark on my heart in regard to Nashville. In fact, I even found myself looking at homes in Music City before we returned to port. After debriefing with Rebecca about the incredible work God did in both our lives over the course of the days on the boat, I finally, and very apprehensively, got around to asking how she felt about Nashville. To my complete surprise, she replied, "Strangely enough, I feel quite open to returning." Apparently, we were in the midst of an act of God.

Within months after arriving home from Alaska, we slowly began trading in our coastal-living dream by splitting time between Tennessee and California. We found a little, nine-hundred-square-foot, two-bedroom, 1920s cottage outside of downtown Franklin, Tennessee. Despite my previous reservations, I quickly found myself falling in love with the rolling hills and lush, green environment of the greater Nashville area. Because of my boyhood fantasies of being Tom Sawyer or Huckleberry Finn, there was a very romanticized vision in my head of the South that I was, for the first time, getting to experience firsthand. Floating down and fishing the local creeks and rivers. Rope swings and tree houses. Chasing fireflies through the tall grass on warm summer evenings. Somebody pour a glass of sweet tea already!

Not to mention, middle Tennessee was a place that more directly aligned with our values and morals. It was a place we were excited to raise our children in. We had been a light in our community in California, which brought a unique sense of purpose. While we had a great community, there is definitely a subconscious draining of your soul that occurs when living in an environment that doesn't support your beliefs. In Tennessee, we more commonly saw other families carrying our same light and it made us feel all the brighter to be surrounded by other believers. Beyond it all, the sense of calling we felt attached to us being in Nashville transcended any desire to be near the beach or in perfect year-round weather. I thoroughly believe walking in the Lord's call is always accompanied by His peace, a peace that transcends understanding (Phil. 4:6–7).

All of a sudden, everywhere we looked, it was like our season of dormancy was giving way to signs of spring. Because of our pain, we had no idea there was anything lying dormant under the surface of the broken soil of our souls. But then little shoots of creative energy emerged from the dust. Almost immediately following the cruise, Rebecca became pregnant again. This little life was the first tangible evidence of a change in our season, and we were beyond ecstatic. We were both excited about stepping back into the arts. It felt risky but right—all at the same time. **But that's where I really think faith lives, right there at the corner of risky and right.**

Risky Faith

When we got married, we boldly (and maybe somewhat naively) said to each other that we knew we were called to a risky, daring, unusual life. We didn't know what all that would entail, we were just certain that God would be writing a unique story with our future. So we stepped back into that complex space that exists outside of our comfort zones and returned to our risky faith.

Risky faith is depending on Jesus because we're doing things we simply could not do on our own. It's taking action based on calling rather than conventional wisdom or practicality. It's stepping up to the plate knowing we don't have what we need to accomplish the task on our own but trusting that God will supply it to us based on His Word, a Holy Spirit nudge, or just a curious question mark. In a way, it's where we must step out of the boat with Peter and walk on the water toward Jesus. Sure, we'll stumble, fall, and sink along the way (again, we cannot do this on our own), but we get out of the boat and know what it's like to have Jesus' hand locked into ours, to behold

His eyes as He holds us and moves us forward into the humanly impossible (Matt. 14:29–31).

Because of all we had experienced to that point, our dependence on Jesus was clear. Without a doubt, we knew we were not enough without Him. Looking back, we could recognize some underlying questions of the heart that we had been wrestling with prior to stepping out in faith:

> *Am I trusting Jesus with my daily life, or am I hanging out in the boat because it's comfortable?*
> *Am I dreaming with God about where He wants me to go and what He wants me to do?*
> *Am I looking for new ways that He wants to use me at my church, in my relationships, and in my parenting, or am I just relying on my old habits and ways?*

If you want to get out of the boat and step into risky faith, we'd encourage you to wrestle with similar questions. We did and ultimately found ourselves trading in our safe little ship for a move across the country. Rebecca jumped back into recording a new album, and I picked up a camera and guitar.

Ultimately, the riskier thing for us would have been to ignore God's call and try to continue forcing ourselves into a life that was no longer meant for us. It's a human tendency to try to accomplish only what we're certain we're capable of and make sure things are perfect before we step out in faith. We want enough money in our bank account and all the boxes to be checked on the list of "what needs to happen before I can ..." But, when you don't take a step because you're fearful of getting out of the boat, you miss the miracle of being on the water with Jesus.

When we seek guidance from God about His direction for our lives, whether it's crystal clear or not, and even though it might not make sense, we must trust the guidance of the Holy Spirit over our logical and practical intuition. When feeling nudges from the Holy Spirit, it must always be tested against the Truth of Scripture, and it's always wise to seek the counsel and wisdom of Godly mentors and trusted Christian community. Proverbs 24:6–7 says, "For by wise counsel you will wage your own war, and in a multitude of counselors there is safety" (NKJV). Get confirmation and then move forward in risky faith.

Back to Music
Rebecca

After moving back to Nashville, we started accepting offers for shows again. From the stage, I publicly shared about our winter season. We still didn't have things all figured out, but God was bringing beauty from the ashes. From my transparency, I sensed audience members finding hope and recognizing they weren't alone in their struggles. Almost tangibly, I could feel the weight people were carrying being lifted. Chains were breaking because Satan is defeated by "the blood of the Lamb and the word of our testimony" (Rev. 12:11). Out of the overflow of the fresh season of spring we were in, new songs began to be written. Melodies were put to poetry and a new album started to form. It seemed I was officially out of retirement!

To top off all of this with the most beautiful of gifts, I became pregnant again and our years of infertility came to an end! I was having a healthy pregnancy, clinging to God each day about everything. I still felt vulnerable, but due to all God had done in my life, I was freshly hopeful. I brought my fears to the Lord. I would pray, "Thank You, Lord, for this day with this baby. Thank You that, right now, I'm pregnant." I had to learn to not let my worries for the future take away from the good that was present at that moment. While there's always an element of pain in life because we live in a broken world, there is still always something to be grateful for.

Thank the Lord, we made it to the end of our pregnancy with another healthy, beautiful baby girl. Just as before, I had another induction because apparently my children like to hang out way beyond their due date. We named her "Imogen," meaning "pure" or "innocent." We loved that her name also teased the word "imagine" and the concept of dreaming, because we were finally dreaming again. Her nickname became "Love Bug" because of her sweet demeanor, and to this day she is still known to us as "Bug." As we held our joyous, happy "love bug," we knew she was a part of our "joy com[ing] in the morning" (Ps. 30:5 ESV).

Though we felt that with Imogen's arrival our winter had fully given way to spring, it wasn't all rainbows and sunshine. There were still challenges along the way. In 2018, our family hit the road with newborn Imogen to join a traveling festival featuring other Christian artists called the "Greatest Hits Live" tour. I felt peaceful about taking part because the strength of my voice was returning, so music didn't seem so threatening anymore. I had a great sound check and dress rehearsal the night before the tour started but woke up the day of the first show sick, in part due to the lack of rest that comes with having an infant. I completely lost my voice and missed the first show. I found myself fighting back against the thought, *I can't do this*. I learned to let it be okay to wobble a bit as I got my singing legs back underneath me.

By way of my brothers, Bethel Music had intersected with my family at a For King and Country show. My dad (who was still managing me) had the idea for me to write and record a worship album with Bethel. We met over the phone and collectively sensed we were meant to create music together. Very shortly after, I began joining them in writing sessions for new music that would be released under Bethel's Heritage imprint.

All this was the start of me returning to music with an open heart and hands full, juggling our growing family and a new version of life in ministry.

Back to Film
Cubbie

Going back to film after fighting the idea for so long felt completely natural. It was like hopping on a bike I hadn't ridden in years. I was in my lane. Full speed ahead. Before, I was dwindling away without direction or vision. But I was now running toward the passion and dreams God had placed in my heart. I was exhilarated and full of inspiration rather than living out Proverbs 29:18, "Where there is no vision, the people perish" (KJV).

Awhile back, my old friend from college and roommate in LA, Kevin (one of the guys at the party where Rebecca and I met who had been scheming to get us together), had sent me a short film script he and his sister had been working on. Kevin and I collaborated on a couple short films in college, and we have talked and dreamed extensively about doing more film projects together. But when he originally sent me the idea, it was in our "winter" and I wasn't in an emotional place to properly receive it. It felt like a mountain that I wasn't ready, or even desired, to climb. However, I was now full of fresh inspiration and ready for a creative adventure. So, after we returned home from the cruise, my first phone call was to Kevin.

"We've gotta make this thing happen," I said, and he agreed. So, we rallied, pooled our resources, called in a bunch of favors, locked down locations and a crew, and made a short film. Seeing the project through from start to finish was incredibly gratifying and confirmed that directing is 100 percent my sweet spot. It is truly the place where all my passions, giftings, and talents converge, and I felt the complete and absolute fulfillment of doing exactly what I am created to do.

There's an indescribable sense of rightness when we're operating at the center of our gifting, almost like our brains work in a different way. When I'm directing, it's like I slip into a different plane of reality. My senses heighten and I simultaneously see the macro and micro implications of every word of dialogue, camera angle, and nuance existing within the frame. I had been missing that connection to a craft. I had been walking backwards, away from what I was meant to be doing. But now, it was clear that I was headed in the right direction.

Next, my sights turned to an idea that was birthed while the world was turned upside down in 2020. As was the case for many of us, a whole array of emotions stirred up in me during that unique moment in time. I found myself deeply troubled by our culture's blatant attack on identity, specifically the outright onslaught on masculinity. Men don't seem to know what it means to be a man anymore. Previous definitions have been labeled toxic, men have been deemed the enemy, and most are left feeling paralyzed to operate according to any former model out of fear of being chastised or canceled.

I felt a deep burden to rise up and challenge these cultural positions that everyone seemed to be bowing to. I desired to create something that would not only be beautifully cinematic and entertaining, but also inspire men to stand up and live, lead, love, honor, and adventure in the way God created them. At that point, the Lord seemed to drop the idea for a TV series in my lap.

The show would explore masculinity and identity from a biblical perspective set to a backdrop of epic adventures. As this concept began to materialize, my mind immediately went to the manliest dude I knew: my dear friend and former roommate Brent, an Alaskan native and former cast member on the History Channel show *Mountain Men*. The idea was that in each episode, we would take a guest who shared our faith—and also held some form of cultural prominence— on an adventure: and explore the question of what it means to be a man who bears the image of the Creator of the universe. As the show progresses outward, the conversation would move inward with the intention of getting to the heart of what makes these guys tick, seeking to understand the foundation of their faith, and decipher what guides and motivates their professional and personal decisions.

The ultimate hope was to inspire men to stop listening to the lies culture has been speaking over them and stand up to be who they were created to be.

We decided to call the show *What is Man*, inspired by Psalm 8:4 that reads, "what is man, that you are mindful of him." While we hit some challenges and roadblocks in the process of putting it together, we were eventually able to shoot the pilot episode in Alaska. As we are writing this book, we are in postproduction on the pilot. Another God-given idea is coming to fruition, and that has been and still is giving me life.

There have been several other projects like music videos, commercials, TV series, and feature films that have come my way in this season. But there hasn't been anything quite as sweet as getting to collaborate on projects with my wife. We had a word spoken over us several times during engagement and early marriage that we would be stronger for the Kingdom together than we were apart. We thoroughly believe this and have actively been pursuing the reality of what this means in the midst of the things the Lord has called us to.

Months before the cruise, I had a dream where Rebecca picked up a guitar and said, "Hey, I want to show you something." She sat down and played a new song for me. She sang it with a guttural passion and a voice that I had never heard come out of her. It was pure, rich, and so full of heart. As she strummed the last chord and looked up at me, I was blown away. Her voice was incredibly strong, unencumbered by the pain or trauma of her past. When I woke up, I couldn't shake the dream or the feeling that God would not only restore her voice but give her a new one. He started to make this dream a reality during her performance on the cruise, but I got to witness firsthand her radical restoration through the process of partnering on her new album.

Chapter 13

FULL-CIRCLE MOMENTS

Rebecca

God really brought our lives and relationship full circle when He began to intertwine our formerly separate careers. As I started to write and record music again, it felt very organic and right to draw Cubbie into the process. I loved seeing him come to life as he jumped back into film. We were both returning to the arts so why wouldn't we take this bold leap together?

Cubbie became the executive producer for my latest album *Kingdom Come* and spoke into everything from songwriting to sounds and production. We had never collaborated on that level before, and it was beautiful to see that Cubbie and I truly were stronger together than apart. There's always tension that arises in a creative process where numerous thoughts are on the table, but even there, we deferred to one another and trusted how we each executed ideas. Our confidence in each other was evident, and we were able to push each other to truly give this album our best.

During the process, my brothers Joel and Luke also came to give their time to my project. I cried when they shared they wanted to contribute because I knew they were so busy with their own music but were still wanting to write and record songs with me. Luke and I worked on *Dawn* together and we all collaborated on *Kingdom Come*. We locked arms together as a family, with even the kids and Cubbie singing background vocals and being in the music video for the title track.

From start to finish, *Kingdom Come* ended up taking a couple of years to create mostly due to the unique challenges that 2020 brought to the world. Over that time, I nursed Imogen between songwriting and recording takes and Cubbie produced while working on other projects and also juggling the kids. On a typical full day with my longtime producer, Tedd T, and many of the members of the Bethel worship community, I would feed Imogen, set her down on the rug for playtime or put her down for a nap in her crib, and then hop back into a writing session. Those years involved a lot of creative scheduling, but God seemingly gave us this long stretch so that we could take the time we needed to learn how to be gracious toward each other as we navigated parenting and work life together.

Cubbie

If I wasn't physically in the studio with Rebecca, I was at home with the kids. I was happy to hold down the home front and enjoyed the newfound partnership I experienced with Rebecca. Despite my dreams about film and TV, I reached a point where I began to wonder if we were meant to focus on one thing and move in tandem. Could this be what "stronger together" was meant to look like? I could support Rebecca's music, we could travel as a family, and I could play when there were live performances. Regardless of the answer to that question at that moment, there were simply not enough hours in the day to focus on anything beyond raising our growing children and finishing the record.

With her new sense of healing and freedom, we had an assumption that returning to music would be smooth going this go-around. The divine nature by which Rebecca was led back into ministry and music left us both a bit surprised to find that in some ways stepping back in was more challenging than we had anticipated. While God didn't completely smooth the path, He did give Rebecca the tools to navigate it better and we had the gift of walking through the challenges together.

I was so proud of Rebecca through the entire recording process. I watched her rediscover her confidence and strength in her voice. Seeing her through the early stages of writing, and watching her step back into recording again, it was like watching her become a whole new person. Even her producer, who had worked on her earliest records, told her that her vocal sound was the strongest it had ever been. Her voice seemed to not just be returning but also being made new.

After we got through the push of the album and the busy years following, Rebecca wanted to pull back a bit to make room for the things we felt the Lord calling me to. I voiced my idea to lay down my personal projects and partner with her full-time. She was resistant. "You can't let go of the dreams God has put in your heart. You can't neglect the giftings He's given you. You need to chase those things." How do you argue with that? I couldn't.

That's when I learned, in a marriage and parenting partnership, sometimes there's give and sometimes there's take.

The Partnership of Parenting
Rebecca

In this season, Cubbie and I were so integrated with our lives that it allowed us to tag team well with our parenting. We were able to anticipate each other's needs and find ways to help each other care for the kids as we also went about our work. We had made a commitment that we wanted to be the ones who primarily cared for our children, no matter how busy our schedules became. We never wanted them to grow up to be bitter about ministry life or think it robbed them of time with their mum and dad. So, even with both of us navigating opportunities, we figured out how to partner in our parenting and invite our children into the journey of our calling as a family. My mum once said soon after I stepped back into music that if Cubbie and I were being faithful to God in what He had called us to do, then there was blessing in that for our children as well. I have held on to this thought when the juggle has been a challenge and I've seen it to be true.

Because we have included our kids as part of our ministry life, they have often partnered with us in prayer. There are many times when I ask them to pray for me before shows and it's beautiful to hear, "God, please give Mommy confidence, bless her show. Please help Mommy to be brave." They remind me that my strength is found in Jesus. It's empowering to be supported by our children because they know they are a part of this mission too. They're on our team. They have even prayed for this book. We love that our kids are beginning to overhear grateful reflections from audience members after my shows.

Often individuals or couples come up to me with a similar and wonderful story ... they are thankful for my music and True Love Waits message from decades past. It changed their lives and the way they related to the opposite sex in dating. One couple just recently shared their love story with me. They met in their twenties and she was his first girlfriend. They have had a wonderful dating and marriage experience, mostly due to their shared beliefs about God and purity. Now they are passing these teachings on to their children. They want their kids to know that holiness is chosen out of a relationship with Jesus, with a simple desire to honor our Father and glorify Him. They believe if their kids will pursue holiness and purity because they genuinely trust that God's way is best—not out of performance, legalism, or to please a church leader—it will bless and protect them.

They want their kids to know that the decision to not have sex outside of marriage will honor God, their future spouse, and even bless their future children. This is EXACTLY what Cub and I believe and want for our kids too. This is the message we want them to overhear.

It really matters what we believe because our faith and our values become our legacy. It's up to us as parents to get on the same page and determine our values. We pass down to our kids what we believe about God and about things like purity, holiness, and God's Word. What are we saying to our kids about holiness, not only through what we speak but how we live? What value do we assign to being set apart for God and living according to His Word? What are we saying to our kids about the importance of honoring Him in our relationships? Our narratives on these topics as parents are writing the beginning pages for our kids' understanding on these matters and the start of their own unique story as well.

When we choose to speak negatively of the church, focus on only the bad and throw the baby out with the bathwater with movements like True Love Waits, or joke about certain aspects of Christianity, we're actually telling our kids at worst that these things are bad and at best that purity, modesty, Christian community, etc. don't really matter. So, we must ask ourselves: What stories do we want to start for our children? Then, we need to begin to communicate these values clearly. We are partners in raising Kingdom-focused kids and it's up to us, as a team, to steward this moment in time with them well.

Cubbie

We noticed a few years into our parenting partnership that our family didn't quite feel complete. It was missing something. Well, someone really. So, we approached the idea that we might want to grow our family again by two more tiny feet.

Because of our miscarriages, there was legitimate fear about trying again. We sought counsel from some very wise friends of ours about whether or not we should. They offered us this insight: "God is generally more definitive about his 'no' than He is about His 'yes.' So, if you don't have a 'no' then maybe you should just leave this in God's hands and see what happens." We decided to take their advice and God placed from His hands into ours another positive pregnancy test. We hadn't found out the gender of the girls before they were born, but this time around, we thought it would be fun to find out. Maybe even try our hand at one of those gender reveal parties!

So, before Gemma's birthday party at our new home in Franklin, Tennessee, Rebecca's sister was given "the secret envelope" with the gender details and she filled a piñata with gender specific color candies. When Gemma hit the piñata, she and all of us partygoers would find out if she was getting a brother or a sister.

As a former baseball player, I was proud of Gemma as she swung and made perfect contact with the piñata. Into the air exploded a shower of blue confections declaring that, for the first time, the Finks were about to welcome a little boy into the family. *A boy!*

While we broke tradition to find out we were having a baby boy, we kept true to keeping our kids' names a secret until their own birthdays. Once again, we were thinking about a unique name. A favorite verse of ours had been Psalm 1:3,

"He shall be like a tree planted by the rivers of water, that brings forth its fruit in its season, whose leaf also shall not wither; and whatever he does shall prosper" (NKJV). What about River? Rebecca and I both loved the symbolism of water and had encountered God in special ways connected to rivers. So, River he became.

What I didn't anticipate was how knowing I was having a little boy would rush back repressed memories from my boyhood and usher in my own healing. I had to pick back up with counseling. There were dark memories I knew I would have to bring into the light to be the father I wanted to be to both my girls, and now my son.

Facing the Trauma

It isn't just good philosophy, counseling, or theology that heals you. Healing comes from realizing that God is with us in our pain, that only He can make sense of our suffering, and that He not only wants to renew our hearts but use our wounds to mend the hearts of others—that brings true restoration.

As a father, I knew I had to bring to God my inability to process my buried emotions and allow Him to place others in my path to help me heal. But now something about having a son motivated me, and I knew I couldn't pass down to him a legacy of manhood that involved being passive about his heart.

Growing up, I did not have, and was never taught, an emotional language. I felt things deeply but I didn't know how to verbalize the things in my heart. My parents were both from an era, and from families, where feelings didn't get talked about much. As a result, very little emotional expression was modeled in my home, and I had no reference point for how to express what I was feeling during my formative years.

I got good at hiding any pain. I constantly surfed, rode my bike, played baseball, and made music. Mostly, people inferred I was a happy kid. And my childhood was truly happy. I had incredibly loving and supportive parents, a very close relationship with my sister, and I always knew home was a safe place.

There was just a sadness that lingered in my soul. In old home videos you can see me, a kid trying to have fun but carrying the weight of the world on his shoulders. I never really figured out how to express the heaviness that hung like a cloud over my life.

Communicating my emotions was something I struggled with until college. I connected with one of my anthropology professors who became a mentor to me. One of the first things he helped me with was to develop an emotional vocabulary. As part of that process, he gave me an assignment to draw a picture of my heart. So I tried. The thing that ended up on the page was basically a chimney-like structure that was turned on its side, with the open cavity bent into view. Instead of being a straight chimney, it was twisted and swirled off into infinity, something reminiscent of an M. C. Escher drawing. Just inside, crouching just beyond where the light was reaching, was a dark figure. You could tell a figure was there, but you couldn't really make out what it was exactly.

In a lot of ways, that was my emotional state: all twisted up, wild, and hard to navigate. Somewhere in my heart was this lingering, dark presence just beyond the shadow line. It was just kind of watching me and putting me in a state of confusion and fear. I had to man up and face the shadow figure of my past so my son would never have to encounter him in his future.

Shortly after arriving in Nashville, I was introduced to a man who, in my opinion, is the perfect blend of intellectual and spiritual. He has a radical understanding of the power of the Holy Spirit along with a deep knowledge and understanding of physiology and psychology. He integrated both sides of mental and spiritual into his process of helping his clients heal from trauma. This man taught me that the mind stores trauma outside of time. So anytime that pain is activated, the mind reverts to the age you were when you experienced it. The idea is to heal that old version of yourself so they are not the ones driving the bus the next time you stumble across or into those memories.

Rebecca volunteered to go with me for my first session. I was nervous because I still sensed the presence of the "shadow figure," but I didn't know what to do with it or how I'd react if I encountered it. This counselor eased my nerves a bit by simply getting to know me. He taught me about the built-in protective mechanisms that God designs in our minds and emotions to enable us to keep going after experiencing something traumatic. The gap in my memories was an example of such protections.

Nearing the end of the session, we walked through a practice that would become familiar. I would close my eyes, he would ask me a series of questions, I would describe the visions that would come to my mind, and he would take furious notes. He'd give his insights back to me at the end, and we would seek the Holy Spirit to help draw any connections to my memories and conclude our time with where God may be leading me.

Within that very first session, I saw myself alone in a nondescript room. From behind me I heard a door open and felt the presence of someone enter the room. Something in me knew this presence was the embodiment of the shadow figure from my drawing. I was immediately gripped with a radical fear that I didn't know I was capable of feeling. In this state of fear and panic, my emotions were unpinned, and I began to cry uncontrollably.

For the first time in years, I was crying. This was a huge deal because I hadn't really cried since I was a kid, when I decided that crying was stupid. But crying isn't stupid. The tears were an incredibly clear indicator that there was something very real and very raw that needed to be dealt with. I needed to cry. I needed Rebecca to see me cry. I needed release so I could find restoration.

In every one of my sessions I would receive incredibly vivid pictures. Early on I tangibly saw my heart as a massive rock wall in the middle of an overgrown garden. Even small glimpses of things would develop into ornate murals that would play out like a movie to help guide and direct me through the journey of discovery God had me on. Every image was incredibly rich and dripping with meaning and insight.

Slowly but surely, I let it all go and began to take steps towards restoration. God transformed that office into a holy room for me to work through my past and pain. I got to know my five-year-old self and started to fill in the missing holes in my memories. Often with weeks between sessions for me to regain the emotional strength to continue to push forward, we finally reached the place I dreaded—but knew we'd have to eventually arrive at—for me to heal: the place where the shadow figure lived.

My counselor opened the session by saying, "I want you to close your eyes and find a place, either recent or in your past, where you felt very close to Jesus. Picture that place." The second I closed my eyes, I immediately saw an image of a willow tree. I had seen that tree before. It was a sacred memory for me from a vision I had in South Africa. I was lying down and worshipping, safe and secure in the presence of Jesus, when I saw a beautiful countryside, rolling hills, and a creek flowing through the middle of it all. On the bank was a gorgeous willow tree with its branches gently moving in the breeze over the flowing water. It was serene. As I turned and looked around, Jesus began walking toward me. We met on the bank and, hand-in-hand, we followed the creek. It was beautiful, and probably the closest I had ever felt with Jesus. I really did not want that image to be tainted by what I might see next.

I tried for about fifteen minutes to push that scene of the willow tree out of my head, but to no avail. Over and over, it returned. I desperately tried to replace it with another image, but I was stuck with the willow. Praying that memory would not be warped, I finally gave in. I told my counselor what I was seeing, and he took his usual notes. "What do you think Jesus wants to show you in this place?" he asked. As if that question was the signal to flip my world upside down, I was now standing with Jesus by the same willow tree, but I was no longer surrounded by lush rolling hills beside the beautiful creek. The willow had become the same tree that grew in my old neighborhood in Bakersfield, right across the street from my old neighbor's house.

Suddenly, I was five years old and uncontrollably crying as I looked at the house. Jesus kept gently drawing my gaze back to Him. As I met His eyes, I was calmed. But each time I tried to muster up the courage to look back at the house, I started bawling again. I couldn't help it. At this point, Jesus got down on one knee to get eye-to-eye with me and placed both His hands on my shoulders. My counselor was prompted to ask, "Is there a version of you from a different era that you would want to help comfort your younger self?" Yes. My sixteen-year-old self who was so on fire in his passion for his newfound faith. He was fearless, and he immediately volunteered without hesitation. And so, sixteen-year-old Cubbie entered the scene.

Now both Jesus and Teenage Cubbie were shielding Child Cubbie, protecting him from both sides. I could now look at the house as the sixteen-year-old, and when I did, I wasn't afraid. He knew exactly what he needed to do. Teenage me turned around like a man on a mission and started walking across the street. As I looked up, I could see a sea of demonic activity in the form of a snake, twisted up and disgusting, swirling and slithering above the house. As I looked ahead to the driveway, I saw him, the shadow figure. It was my neighbor, and he was standing just outside the garage. As I paced closer, I realized it was just a strange cardboard cutout of him. I chuckled because I had been deathly afraid of this man for so long and came to find out he was just a puppet, not something to be afraid of.

Disregarding him, I entered the house to find that everything was completely still, eerily frozen in time. I proceeded to do a quick walk around. I remembered being in the house. I had eaten meals there. I had played with the daughter there. I pushed on, walked down the hallway, and looked into the bedroom. There. That's where things happened. I knew it by the way the bed was unmade, and the room was dark except for the light shining from one small lamp in the corner. On the dresser sat a camera. At the scene, my heart ached for the five-year-old little boy who was forced to be in that room.

As I turned to leave, I took stock in the fact that this house was a place I was familiar with. A place I didn't want to be familiar with, so I had to forget it to survive. I could see the space for what it was: a place Satan controlled. But I had protection now from the Holy Spirit, so I was not affected by the darkness. No longer afraid and ready to close the door on the past that haunted me, I walked out of the house.

As I crossed the street back to the tree, I found Jesus still kneeling eye-to-eye with five-year-old Cubbie. At the arrival of my teenage self, Jesus looked up. With a tear in His eye, Jesus embraced me with the most loving, warm, real, intimate hug I'd ever experienced. As we embraced, I felt five-year-old Cubbie fuse together with sixteen-year-old me, becoming one. And that was it.

You may be wondering do I now know what all really happened to me? My honest answer is, "No, not fully." I can speculate, but it remains in question if I should keep pressing into this scene. Truthfully, I'm not sure if I want to know more about the details of what all took place. But I am certain that through the glimpses and pieces that I've been able to recall, God has offered me unbelievable healing. I have a new level of understanding and compassion for myself as a child. I feel new freedom to grow even closer to Rebecca and access Jesus more freely. Also, the Holy Spirit strengthened me to do something that I previously felt was emotionally impossible. Through that vision I saw Jesus look into my eyes. Now, I can walk in that same divine authority with my focus set on God as I encounter other problems on behalf of myself or others.

I don't share all of this because I want you to think I've done anything worth applauding or to give you a wild story. I'm vulnerable because I feel prompted and almost obligated to share this on behalf of anyone who needs to hear a testimony of the great work Jesus can do. We have the Christ-given ability to break the power of darkness and bring healing, even in the most traumatic or painful moments of our lives and in the lives of others.

When we have children, we all have flashbacks to memories from our own childhoods. Some are great. For me those sweet memories are of baseball games, campouts with my friends at the beach, doing art projects with my mom, laughing with my sister, and surfing with my dad. As you now clearly know, some of my memories are dark and tainted. **We all have a mix of both good and bad as we look back on our lives, and ultimately, we get to decide whether we're going to live from the victory we have in Christ or to play the victim.**

In that counseling session, I got to see both my childhood and teenage self. It made me stand taller in the victory I have in Christ and wonder what I would say to my younger self about what I know now. What kind of things will I someday say to my son? I came up with a little something like this:

"Hey. I know as a young man it seems like you need to have it all together. *Be strong. You are going to be a man, after all.* But the reality is that your strength isn't found in being able to numb your heart or have thick skin. You'll discover that your real strength will be found when you decide to truly open your heart and trust God with your story—every piece of it. I know you won't always be able to see it, but Jesus will never leave your side. When you're fighting, He's fighting with you and for you.

"The measure of a man isn't how tough he is, but it's the legacy he leaves. So keep letting God write your story. In those pages filled with both celebrations and struggle, adventure and grit, you too are leaving behind an instruction guide for your children and their children on how to seek God and fight their battles. Make your story count. In the end, that's what really matters."

While I can't actually go back and talk with my childhood self, I did get to talk to a younger version of Rebecca. Here's how ...

Chapter 14

WALKING TOGETHER IN THE NEW DAY

Rebecca

Having a movie written and filmed about the most influential years of your life story is a wild experience. We moved into the production for *Unsung Hero* soon after the *Kingdom Come* album released. Writer and director Richard Ramsey extensively interviewed me for the script. When it came time to finalize the writing side of things, I was both excited about the journey with the film and Cubbie's involvement, but anxious too as it hit very close to home. I leaned on the instincts of the amazingly creative people on the project knowing that my brother Joel, a director and writer on the project, and Cubbie as a producer and part of the directing team, would have my back and protect this part of my story. I didn't even read the script before they started. It was all a surprise for me as it unfolded.

The preproduction and actual shooting sent Cubbie and the team to the set in Louisville, Kentucky, for about six weeks. Homeschooling our kids made it easy for us to travel back and forth to be with him. We stayed at a rental house and I was happy to be at "home" creating a routine for them, while also occasionally getting to watch Daddy do his thing. It wasn't the best idea to bring the kids on set all the time, though, because they were young and quite hard to keep quiet. So, outside of my half day on set to shoot my role as a flight attendant in the film, I mostly created a sense of normalcy at the Airbnb and we cheered on Dad in his incredible work.

Again, I could see how God used our similar passions to help us support one another. While I had never been a producer or director, I had spent my fair share of time on film sets and understood the pressure Cubbie was under. I did what I could to help him carry the weight. We were in this together.

Premiere

The *Unsung Hero* premiere night was held at a beautiful theater in Nashville called The Fisher Center on April 15, 2024. The whole Smallbone clan attended along with our spouses. We smiled for photographers out of genuine excitement for the movie and offered heartfelt interviews to the media. It was a truly epic moment!

The environment felt at once familiar and new to me. I've done quite a lot of red-carpet events and interviews with a ton of people and media outlets with their flashing cameras. It also felt a little like a family reunion because I knew many of the people there so well. What was entirely new was that this event was about my family, and we had all made something together. This was also the first time Cubbie and I were being interviewed as a couple. Up to this point, I had experienced red carpets and interviews alone. Finally, we were hand-in-hand, answering questions and helping put a movie out into the world. It was a new season for Cubbie and I that was sparked by my family's story.

One of the hardest things in my career as a music artist is how lonely it can be. Years before the movie release, a documentary interviewer asked me what I thought about my brothers Joel and Luke performing music together as For King and Country. I responded with something along the lines of, "I am so proud of them. They're good men. And it's so beautiful to see good men in a position of leadership thriving in their work and influencing a generation." The interviewer bounced back a question that made me so emotional I had to stop answering mid-sentence. "Is there anything about their journey that you wish would have been a part of your story too?" The thing that I have felt envious of about my brothers is that they've had each other, sharing the pressure of the spotlight. With my music, I'm a solo artist. I'm so relational and team oriented that having someone else to walk this road with me would have been way easier and so much less lonely. Thinking of this, I had to pause and weep for a minute or two.

But at the premiere, I was finally not alone. Walking down the carpet with Cubbie, taking the interview questions as a team, I experienced the joy of partnership in the spotlight. Unlike how intimidating Nashville crowds can sometimes be, the whole night everyone seemed ready to receive us with a warm embrace. People were not there to be critical; they were cheering us on. The communal moment of the beginning of the movie premiere and on through the viewing was precious and beautiful, redemptive, and sweet.

After the film finished and the credits rolled, there was a standing ovation. My family started moving into the aisles and everyone was saying, "Come on. Let's go!" Nobody even told me where we were going. I soon realized we were headed toward the stage in front of the screen. With the crowd still cheering, I stood with my family in front of seventeen hundred people at the biggest premiere that Lionsgate Entertainment Company has ever had. As I looked out, I could see so many of our people and community. I could see the full cast and crew. It was a crazy moment, one I tried to soak in because I knew it was extremely special.

Joel then asked for the people who had been in our lives from those earliest of days to stand. To their feet rose Kay and Ed Smith, who dropped groceries on our doorstep and supported us so much in our season of lack when we first came to the US. And there stood John and Luanne Mohr, the family that gave us a car at their Thanksgiving dinner. That moment seeing all the people who were characters in our very real story of God providing and performing the miraculous was so powerful that it nearly brought me to tears. The support from these people from then until now, thirty years later, was overwhelming. Needless to say, the *Unsung Hero* premiere was a night I will never forget.

Cubbie

Reading early iterations of the *Unsung Hero* script, I had a deep sense that this film would usher in healing and redemption, not only for those who would eventually watch the film, but for Rebecca. I witnessed waves of that redemption wash over her through the production process, through the film's completion and release, and I know the Lord is still in the process of using it to bring continued healing for her. What took me a bit by surprise was the healing I would experience as a result of being a part of producing this film.

It's quite a unique and profound opportunity to get to make a movie about the life of your wife. I got to be a part of choosing the cast, finding wardrobe and locations, guiding actors through actions and dialogue, and recreating the stories I had only heard Rebecca tell me about. That's all part of the joy and fun of filmmaking, but there was a part of the process that I didn't anticipate being as impactful as it was.

Not only was I able to watch scenes play out on a small director's monitor, but I was able to step into them and interacted with Rebecca's younger self. In a way similar to how I visited five-year-old Cubbie in my most traumatic moments, I was given the gift of putting my arm around Rebecca's younger self and comforting her in some of her most vulnerable times. I got a glimpse of her surroundings in those moments and even saw a picture of the way the Holy Spirit resided in those situations. I was gifted with a much deeper and richer perspective of the things she walked through, which only grew my love and empathy for her. The entire process was cathartic and, in a way, felt like a form of therapy. I don't think I made it through a single day of production without getting emotional and tearing up.

In the final phases of editing the film, we began doing test screenings. There's a science to the whole process where you hire a company who assembles a completely random, non-biased audience to watch the movie and give honest feedback. It felt like a triumph when rooms full of people wept where I wept and laughed at the humor woven throughout the story. We went through this process several times with different audiences. It was a unique experience each time because every audience carries its own particular personality. You almost see the film through a different lens depending on the audience you're with. Feeling each group receive the story in the way we hoped it would land, and getting to ride the highs and lows of your wife's family story, is a feeling like no other.

While the film went on to be very well received nationwide, which was beyond encouraging, the greatest success to me was the feedback and stories we heard from the people who watched the movie. What we heard overwhelmingly was that this was a film that encouraged fathers, mothers, and children to rally together, stand on their faith, and be reminded of God's powerful design and purpose for the family. Audiences were gently moved toward the healing and redemptive arms of Jesus. It was a Kingdom success. Kingdom success is the greatest success.

THE LOVE THAT'S LASTING EVER

Rebecca

At the beginning of this book, you caught a behind-the-scenes look at me walking offstage, full of fear. Alone. But here at the end, you find Cubbie and I walking out onto the red carpet at the *Unsung Hero* premiere full of hope, hand-in-hand.

I pray that if you have ever found yourself in similar shoes, feeling like you must climb your mountains by yourself, that you now see what was revealed to me—you are never, ever alone. You have been found by God's true love. A love that will never leave.

Because God's character is lasting ever, we can know for certain:

- We are SEEN in the secret places of our lives and pain (Ps. 139).
- God has HEARD every prayerful longing of our heart and will answer in His time. Until then and ongoing, He offers Himself as more than enough (1 John 5:14–15).
- When we're HELD by God, He's not holding us back but is setting us free and offering His comfort (Ps. 63:8).
- We are intimately KNOWN by God. Even with our imperfections and wrestling during

suffering seasons, He cares for us and chooses
us as His sons and daughters (Jer. 1:5).
• We are LOVED ...

In every moment of our lives, we are truly and deeply LOVED and never alone. God partners with us and leads us by the hand into the unknown, wanting us to know that together with Him, we can face anything.

Cubbie and I are incredibly blessed that you have chosen to journey with us through this book. It has been both stretching and defining in our faith life and story. We have told you of our journey of God's TRUE LOVE finding us young in life. We've shared about being found by romance, a covenant love with each other. And then we opened up about God's redemptive love finding us again and again when hardship struck—hope restored each time.

We pray our words have encouraged you to reflect on your own story—how God is constantly working—and that our stories are calling you up, equipping you to be brave enough to fight for your faith and family in a culture that will tell you to bail when things get hard. We pray that you feel inspired to dream again about the future. We hope you long to go on a grand adventure with God to places where you will see Him do things in your life and the lives of others that you would never think of or accomplish on your own.

When we talk about dreaming with God and being open to new adventures with Him by living a risky faith, we speak from *recent* experience! Within the last year, the landscape of our lives has nearly completely changed—for the better. Recently, I was gently convicted by the Holy Spirit that I had idols of control, fear, and people pleasing. Then I felt God's loving voice calling me out from living under them. Cubbie and I are now more intentional about our emotional, mental, and spiritual health. That has given us access to more freedom, peace, and joy.

We have found ourselves again in a new season, this one full of new dreams and possibilities—especially creative endeavors. But to remain intentional, we're asking God to reveal what are healthy "no's," so we have space for our best "yeses" as a family. We have simplified our lives in many ways, one of which is homeschooling full-time. (Which I am aware to many does not sound like simplifying, but to us it does!) I've been approached to write more music and received offers to partner with people to create it. Producers and writers have come to Cubbie with film and TV ideas. Then out of the blue, a friend encouraged us to write a book about our journey, and it inspired us to create these pages you are reading. We knew saying "yes" to sharing our stories was important because we felt a sense of urgency to infuse hope in a time of heavy discouragement for many. Our lives are not pain free or all sorted and dialed— we are sure that you've seen that.

In fact, in some parts of life, there is joy-threatening pain. But through it I know God is inviting a deeper dependence on Him than I've personally ever known. We're still living in a hard, gritty world but, I dare say, with a new confidence, freedom, and hope because the pain of our lives has uncovered a more refined *true love*, relationally and especially spiritually.

I urge you to hear you are truly loved by God and believe it not because it sounds pretty but because I need you to know that even in great hardship, He is working on your behalf. I know this to be true because I've lived it. Sometimes holy things are hard things, and Cubbie and I know without a doubt that if you choose to dig your feet into the solid foundation of Jesus Christ, you won't be moved. The clouds will part. Dawn will break. And you will see His goodness, kindness, and glory.

God's love for you is lasting ever. Let that truly sink in! As a result, you and I are given strength to make commitments to Him and others that are also *lasting*. So keep going and fighting for your faith and relationships. Don't give up! Through our story, and as you write your own with God, we hope you feel us linking arms with you and hear us cheering you on. We are in this *together*.

So my dear brothers and sisters, stand strong. Do not let any-
thing change you. Always give yourselves fully to the work of our
Lord Jesus, for you know your work in the Lord is never wasted.
(1 Cor. 15:58)

Cubbie

Being this candid about my life was honestly pretty hard. I like to keep to myself. But I've sensed God prompting me to tell my story, knowing it is not my story but in fact His story that He has given me the gift of stewarding for His glory. Furthermore, I've felt a Holy Spirit nudge to talk about my trauma because there are so many of us that need to know we're not alone. Remaining silent in our hurt continues to give the enemy victory, but there is power and healing in the process of bringing it into the Light. Despite what we see from our limited view through the things that have happened to us, we are loved by God and His love is lasting ever. It's always been there, even before we discovered it, and eternal love is not going anywhere.

I like how the apostle Paul in writing Romans 8:37–39 almost sounds like he's releasing a battle cry when he says, "No, in all these things we are more than conquerors through him who loved us. For I am sure that neither death nor life, nor angels nor rulers, nor things present nor things to come, nor powers, nor height nor depth, nor anything else in all creation, will be able to separate us from the love of God in Christ Jesus our Lord."

He is so confident in the love he's received from Jesus that he knows it can conquer literally anything that life may throw at him. I pray one day to be as bold as Paul. In my life, I too have discovered that God's love, should we choose to remain in it, can withstand and overcome the darkest trauma, depression, disease, struggle, and even death. In time, these things were replaced for me with healing, a loving wife, a family, a hope for the future, and the ability to dream big again.

Rebecca and I have in no way, shape, or form figured everything out. It's tempting to finish with a "and they lived happily ever after." As a musician and filmmaker, this would offer the resolution and sense of resolve my heart wants to hear. However, you and I both know life does not offer us constant bliss. While there are certainly moments of it, hardship will inevitably come again. But what I can say in full confidence is this: the growth, lessons, and perspective gained on the other side of hardship are invaluable. My biggest takeaway from what we've deemed our winter season, is that it was actually the pain of that period that prompted both of us to venture down the road toward healing. If life was breezy, we would have had no reason or desire to explore those places. While the Lord hates to see His children hurt, pain is never without purpose.

While we can't offer you "happily ever after," we can point you toward God's love that is lasting ever. It's that love that will allow both us and you to endure, press on, and finish our lives here well before we get to enter our heavenly home.

As I have been afforded the opportunity to reflect on and relive so many moments of my life over the course of the last several months, I have had one overwhelming takeaway ... God is so good. His ways are so perfect. And I can wholeheartedly trust Him with all of who I am. It is my prayer that you have a similar takeaway.

As you close this book, hear this: Life will change but God will not. When curveballs are thrown our way, when Satan shoots fiery darts in our direction, may we remember the words of the great King David when he stated in Psalm 16:8, "I have set the LORD always before me; because he is at my right hand, I shall not be shaken" (ESV).

Finally, I would like to offer you something. I received these words at the conclusion of one of my sessions in the process of facing my trauma. It is not scripture, but I believe what I heard was inspired by the Holy Spirit. For anyone walking through hurt and pain, past or present, I believe these words are for you as well. I pray they encourage your heart as they did mine. As Jesus firmly held my shoulders and knelt on one knee to be eye-to-eye with my five-year-old self, this is what I saw and heard. May you see and hear from the Holy Spirit.

> *See the hurt and empathy in Jesus' eyes. He's so sorry. He didn't intend or want this for you, but He is with you. He is compassionately holding you. Feel the warmth and comfort of His embrace and feel a oneness with His heart and soul. Jesus knows you. He sees you. He loves you. He's so sorry that this happened. You are not alone. You were never alone. He knows the hairs on your head, and the hurt and pain in your heart. He sees it. He understands it. He empathizes with it. He is with you. Then, now, and forever.*

Go in the *lasting ever* peace and grace of our loving Father and Savior. Amen.

> *Lord, I'm so tired in this fight*
> *Tired of waking up with no end in sight*
> *I feel I've got so little left*
> *I know that I've come to the end of myself*
> *Help me hold on*
> *Cling to You 'til I see the sun*

Held by Your love, I sing alleluia
You're lifting my heart as I lift my hands
Safe in Your love, I sing alleluia
You're healing my heart as I lift my hands

Water the garden of my life
With every sorrow, every tear that I've cried
Redeem this winter for Your good
Lord, show Your power as only You could
Help me hold on
Cling to You 'til I see the sun,

Held by Your love, I sing alleluia
You're lifting my heart as I lift my hands
Safe in Your love, I sing alleluia
You're healing my heart as I lift my hands

Even in the darkness, even when it's hardest
You are faithful and You bring the dawn
On every mountain, I'll sing it even louder
You are faithful and You bring the dawn

"Dawn" by Rebecca St. James, Tedd Tjornhom,
Luke Smallbone, and Seth Mosley[10]

NOTES

1. Rebecca St. James, "Little Bit of Love," *Rebecca St. James*, ForeFront Records, 1994.

2. Rebecca St. James, "Psalm 139," *Wait for Me*, ForeFront Records, 2003.

3. Compassion International, "About Compassion International," accessed September 17, 2024, www.compassion.com/about/about-us.htm.

4. Francis Brown, Samuel Rolles Driver, and Charles Augustus Briggs, eds., *Old Testament Hebrew Lexicon—New American Standard*, "Miqlat," Bible Study Tools, accessed September 17, 2024, www.biblestudytools.com/lexicons/hebrew /nas/miqlat.html#:~:text=Miqlat%20Definition,refuge%2C%20asylum.

5. Rebecca St. James, "Wait for Me," *Transform*, ForeFront Records, 2000.

6. Rebecca St. James, "I Can Trust You," *If I Had One Chance to Tell You Something*, ForeFront Records, 2006.

7. *Shadowlands*, directed by Richard Attenborough (United States: Savoy Pictures, 1993).

8. I got the idea for this conversation from Justin Whitmel Earley's *Habits of the Household* (Zondervan, 2021).

9. Rebecca St. James, "You Make Everything Beautiful," *I Will Praise You*, Reunion/Beach Street/Essential, 2011.

10. Rebecca St. James, "Dawn" with Luke Smallbone, *Dawn*, Heritage, 2020.